THE STORY OF
ROTTON PARK

THE STORY OF
ROTTON PARK

Margery Elliott

BREWIN BOOKS

First published by
Brewin Books Ltd, 56 Alcester Road,
Studley, Warwickshire B80 7LG in 2019
www.brewinbooks.com

© Margery Elliott 2019

All rights reserved.

ISBN: 978-1-85858-541-3

The moral right of the author has been asserted.

A Cataloguing in Publication Record
for this title is available from the British Library.

Typeset in Haarlemmer MT Std
Printed in Great Britain
by 4edge Ltd.

CONTENTS

	Introduction	vii
1	The Lodge	1
2	The Garden	12
3	The Farm	19
4	The Reminiscences of Miss May Nicholds	26
5	The Early History of Rotton Park	31
6	Map 2, the 1825 Reservoir Map	36
7	Joseph Gillott's 1851 Purchase of Rotton Park	39
8	Maps 3 to 8 and Map 10	41
9	Map 9 and the 1911 Sale Catalogue	48
10	The Chesshires	51
11	The Dockers	57
12	How James Turner came to buy the Lodge	62
13	The Turners	65
14	Stanton Marsh and Developments, 1931-1934	84
15	The Elliotts	90
16	The Tennis Club, the Squash Club and Developments, 2013-2014	114
17	Rotton Park Road Station	119
18	Some Distinguished Inhabitants of Rotton Park	122
	Conclusion	127

An aerial view of Rotton Park Road, Selwyn Road and Wheatsheaf Road taken in c2000. Supplied by Ken Greaves.

INTRODUCTION

Most people who know the Hagley Road area of Edgbaston, Birmingham, will know where Rotton Park Road is. It was cut, the southern half of it across fields and the rest on the line of an old lane or field path, between 1825 and 1828, while Rotton Park Reservoir (later renamed Edgbaston Reservoir) was being constructed. It runs approximately northwards in two straight stretches for nearly a mile from Hagley Road to Dudley Road and is a continuation of Norfolk Road, with which it now shares the road number B4129.

From Hagley Road it slopes downwards, crossing Portland Road at an angle, as far as the entrance on the right to Edgbaston Reservoir. At this low point the Rotton Park Brook crosses under it in a culvert and flows into the Reservoir. The road then climbs to its highest point (549 feet above sea level) by house 143A. It veers slightly towards the east just before crossing Gillott Road, runs fairly level as far as the City Road crossing and then descends steadily to meet Dudley Road. Apart from the playing fields on its western side between Gillott Road and City Road, it has for many years had continuous housing on both sides. Recently, houses and new roads have been created on these former playing fields opposite Hallewell Road.

But in the mid-1850s there were only two houses in the road, apart from a possible few near the two ends. These were a Farm with its outbuildings on the eastern side just south of where Gillott Road is now and a large Victorian Gothic house, called simply 'Rotton Park' by its first owner, but later known as 'Rotton Park Lodge', which stood back from the road in over an acre of garden just south of the Farm. I shall hereafter refer to this house as '**the Lodge**', with a capital L, and to its medieval predecessor on the same site as '**the old lodge**' with a lower-case first letter. The Farm was built in the early 1720s. The Lodge, built in about 1852, had a long drive which ran southwards through its garden and then through a field, before turning to the right and opening into Rotton Park Road just north of where Selwyn Road is now.

Rotton Park itself is known to have been a hunting park, probably a deer park, in the 'Foreign' part of Birmingham as early as 1305. It belonged to the **de Bermingham** family, the Lords of the Manor. The old lodge, originally inhabited by a park keeper, became a second farmhouse after Rotton Park was 'disparked' (i.e., made available for agriculture) in 1553. All except one of the early maps which I have examined show the Farm and the old lodge as the only two buildings in the area, calling them jointly either 'Rotton Park Lodge' or just 'The Lodge'. Rotton Park is spelt as Rotten Park on many of these old maps. I have found no explanation of what the name 'Rotton' means which convinces me ('cheerful farm' is one suggestion) and I have not found any connection between the Park and the Rotton family of Stratford House, near Highgate, Birmingham.

Rotton Park had been owned since 1610 by successive generations of the Perrott family of Belbroughton in Worcestershire, some of whom had sold off parcels of land around its borders by 1851. The remaining 500 acres were sold in 1851 by the then owner, Charles Noel, the grandson of Mrs Catherine Noel, née Perrott. The purchaser was the pen-nib manufacturer Joseph Gillott, who intended to develop Rotton Park as an upper middle-class residential district.

John Chesshire, the surveyor and land agent who acted for Mr Gillott, bought the old lodge and its grounds for himself. He had the old lodge demolished, built a new house which he called simply 'Rotton Park' on its site and lived there from about 1852. After his death in 1894 his house was bought in 1895 by the industrialist and county cricketer Frank Dudley Docker, who restored the word 'Lodge' to its name. He stayed only until 1902. The third and last owner was my maternal grandfather James Richard Turner, a builder by trade, who moved in during 1905 and died there in 1933. All three owners eventually became Justices of the Peace.

The Farm, empty after 1930, stood until 1931, though most of its outbuildings and all of the fields behind it had gone long before that, leaving just the farmhouse with small front and back gardens, the farmyard (and also the back drive which it shared with the Lodge) behind a high brick wall with a slatted double gate onto Rotton Park Road. A speculative builder called Stanton Marsh bought it, pulled all the buildings down in 1931 and built a pair of fairly large semis and one detached house, all with garages, on the site.

James Richard Turner and his wife Emily Jane had four daughters, two sons and a fifth daughter, in that order. When, in 1907, his second daughter, Amy Winifred, became engaged to marry Edwin Elliott, James had a house, 135 Rotton Park Road, built for them. This was on the northernmost part of a plot of land running southwards from his own garden down to the Selwyn Road corner which he had bought at auction in 1906 for £3,350. My parents were married on 25 July 1908 and 135 was their home until 1934. Their three children, all born at home, were Kathleen (Kay), Maxwell (Max) and myself. As children we were lucky enough to have the run of the Lodge's big garden and were frequently in and out of the Lodge itself to see our grandparents. Kay (born 5 April 1910) was

Introduction

the eldest and I (born 26 July 1919), was the youngest of their seven grandchildren. Max (born 8 August 1914) was a delicate and much-loved child with Down's Syndrome. He died of pneumonia in 1927 at the age of twelve. I am the Turners' last surviving grandchild and I must be the only person now alive with detailed memories (and photos) of the Lodge and its garden and admittedly less detailed memories of the Farm. These two historic houses and the people who lived in them deserve to be recorded. That was my reason for deciding to write this book, which has turned out to be both a history of Rotton Park in general and a study of some of the families who lived in this particular part of it up to 1934.

According to my mother, the Lodge had for some unknown reason been built without a damp-proof course. In his old age my grandfather had spent little or nothing on its upkeep, so it was damp and no longer marketable as a dwelling-house after his death. His six surviving offspring, to whom he had bequeathed the house and garden, decided to put them on the market as a building site. The builder who had already bought the Farm, Stanton Marsh, bought the Lodge at auction, demolished it and built two parallel rows of houses, one row in Rotton Park Road and the other in Wheatsheaf Road. These houses all have long, narrow gardens, some of which have mature trees in them.

Much of this book is therefore about the area bounded by Rotton Park Road, Selwyn Road, Wheatsheaf Road and Gillott Road, but my investigations have turned up so much interesting information about the whole of the Rotton Park area, including Edgbaston Reservoir, that I have included this. I have tried to make each chapter complete in itself, which is why so many facts appear more than once in different chapters.

Neither my sister Kay nor I had been interested in history at school, but after Kay took early retirement in 1962 she began to study the history of Rotton Park and became fascinated by it. Sadly, she died in 1970, aged only 60, leaving all her papers, maps and photos to me. I have continued to study the area from where she left off.

In order to find out how to go about writing a book like this, I first completed a two-year part-time course of 'Birmingham Studies', submitting as my final effort a fairly long illustrated essay entitled 'Rotton Park Lodge and the Farm'. I went on to gain a Diploma of Higher Education in 'Local, Family and Community History'. Both of these courses were run by the now sadly discontinued Centre for Lifelong Learning of the University of Birmingham. It has taken me a *very* long time to get this book into print but at 98 years of age I have slowed down. I no longer drive, so I have visited Rotton Park only rarely in recent years.

I acknowledge with gratitude the help, encouragement and well-deserved criticism given to me by my course Director Peter Leather and all the other University of Birmingham staff members who taught us.

I dedicate the book to the memory of my sister Kathleen Elliott. She was a wonderful older sister and friend, well-known in Birmingham as the Principal of her own Edgbaston Secretarial Training College at 529 City Road and also as the highly efficient Chairman, Honorary Secretary, Treasurer or Committee member of many organisations. I am grateful to her for introducing me to such a fascinating subject as the history of Rotton Park.

Many people have known for a long time that I am writing a book about Rotton Park and I apologise to them for keeping them waiting for so long to see it. It is not easy to finish a book containing photos and maps with a tendency to fall asleep while working on it!

Margery Elliott

Chapter 1

THE LODGE

I have been unable to discover who the architect and builders of the Lodge were or to find any original plans of it, as these details did not have to be registered when the house was built in about 1852. So my friend the Harborne architect Ann Levitt, working from interior and exterior photos, maps and my memories, has constructed tentative plans for me which we both hope are about 90% correct. Nobody ever seems to have taken any photos of the north side of the house (the least interesting side architecturally) and only one of the oldest photos of the Farm, taken when the trees between the Lodge and its kitchen garden were not in leaf, shows the whole western side of the Lodge, but not very clearly, so Ann had to use a certain amount of imagination along with her architectural knowledge.

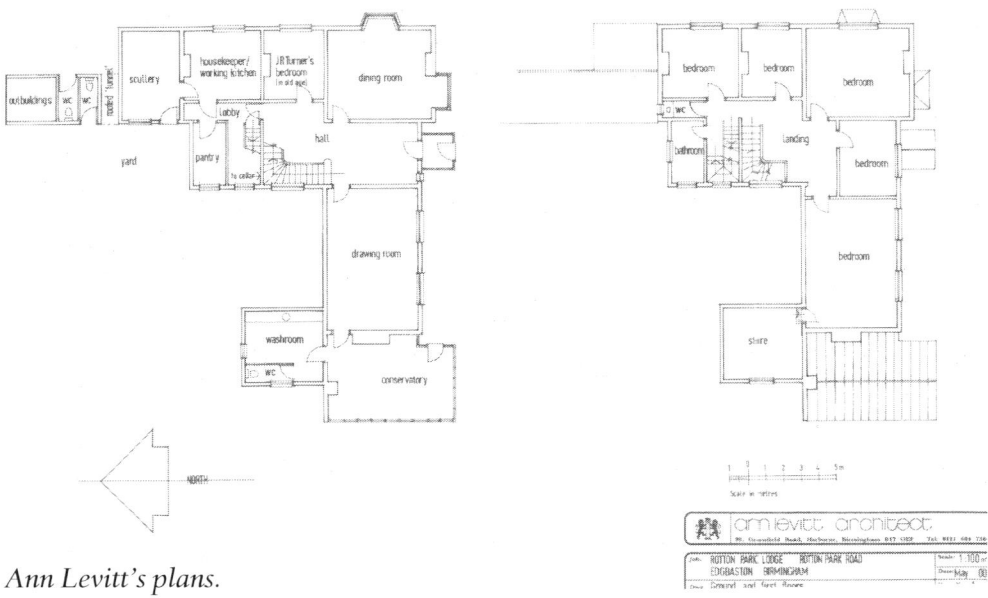

Ann Levitt's plans.

Two early photos of the Lodge, taken around 1894 (from May Nicholds).

1. The Lodge

The house, one of the largest ones on the Rotton Park estate and certainly the one with the biggest garden (apart from the former Summerfield House and its garden which became Summerfield Park in 1876) was built of brick covered with pebbledash and had a slate roof. The most noticeable external features were the 'hood mouldings' over the casement windows on the ground and first floors and the perforated barge-boards on the ends of the gables, both common in houses of that period. I know of quite a few surviving Victorian Gothic houses in various parts of Birmingham with similar features.

The Lodge was eventually numbered 143 Rotton Park Road, but because of its big garden our house, although next door to it, was 135. The front of the Lodge faced south. The drive (shortened by my grandfather) was where the semi-detached house 143 and its garden are now. The open gateway was just south of the road's highest point. The drive curved to the left towards the house and then divided into two by the conservatory. The left-hand branch went round the conservatory to the back yard, the path to the kitchen garden, the coach house and the Lodge's scullery door. The wider right-hand branch ran past the front door and the dining room and ended near the side lawn, where it adjoined a narrow path at right angles to it along the eastern side of the house.

The large separate coach house, by my time used as a garage, stood in the back yard immediately to the east of the farmhouse. Unfortunately no photo of it can be found. It was wide enough to hold three or four cars side by side and it had been built later than the Lodge itself. It had sliding doors, a hayloft, a pitched roof and a dovecot with a weather-cock on top. It was still standing in 1975 but it was later reduced to a single-storey building.

The Lodge's outer front door was never locked during the daytime. It led into a small porch with multi-coloured obscured glass window panes on both sides and above the door. (These must have been added by my grandfather, as the porch's sides are open to

Kathleen canvassing in Harborne for her grandfather in 1912.

Above: The front of the Lodge, just before demolition, 1934.

Left: The hall and the front staircase, 1934.

Bottom: Lord Mayor's landau outside the Lodge, 1906/1907.

1. The Lodge

the weather on the earliest photos.) An inner glazed front door led into the hall, which had a floor of squares of white marble laid so that their diagonals were parallel to the walls. There was a hall stand on the left, next to the inner front door and the small Gothic window. A grandfather clock which showed the phases of the moon as well as the time stood towards the back on the right. On the walls I also remember a 'banjo' barometer, a black-and-white engraving of William Holman Hunt's painting 'The Light of the World', a large framed photograph of my sister, aged not quite three, canvassing successfully for her grandfather in Harborne when he put up for the City Council in 1912 and a telephone.

This, in a wooden case attached to the wall, had two mushroom-shaped bells on top, a trumpet in front to talk into, a handle which had to be cranked before telling the lady operator at the Edgbaston exchange (in Bellis Street) what number you wanted to call and an earpiece on a flex hanging from a U-shaped hook on the right. Relatively few private houses had telephones in the 1920s. The phone number was Edgbaston 1054.

A baize-covered door separated the hall from the kitchen quarters. The front staircase, with a window on its left-hand side, went up only as far as the first floor.

My uncle David Royce took a photo of the Lodge's frontage and some interior photos in 1934, just before the Lodge was demolished. Unfortunately he thought of doing so only after all the furniture had been sold and removed. Noteworthy was the statue of a woman holding a torch at the foot of the front staircase.

The Lodge was built before electricity came to Birmingham in the 1890s and must originally have been lit by gas (the 1911 sale catalogue mentions a gas pipe which ran under the Farm's land and supplied the Lodge). A single gas-fired radiator stood in the hall, next to the staircase. There were enough chimney-pots to show that all of the main rooms except the one leading off the master bedroom must have had fireplaces.

To the right of the hall at the front of the house was the dining room. It had two bay windows, an original one at the eastern end

The statue at the foot of the front staircase, 1934.

and another which my grandfather must have had fitted into the front wall to the right of the fireplace. His rocking-chair and footstool stood by this window and I remember him spending much of the day sitting there and reading the *Birmingham Post*. Between the door and his chair there was a reed organ, complete with pedal-board, which my uncle Wilfrid used to play. If the pedal-board was in use, a second person was needed to pump air with a lever. If not, the player could pump with his feet, as on a harmonium.

Against the left-hand wall there was a long sideboard. This was covered by an unbleached linen runner with red or blue scalloped edges, embroidered by my grandmother. Standing on this were a biscuit barrel, a fruit bowl and several other pieces of blue Wedgwood Jasperware with white human figures in relief on it, a collecting box for the London Missionary Society and a bottle of Montserrat lime juice (the strongest drink allowed in this teetotal household). In the middle of the room there was a large dining table, only half of which, nearer to the door, was used for meals, as four of the five daughters had married and left home by my time. The other half was covered by a dark green chenille tablecloth, on which there were piles of my grandfather's business papers and letters, held down by paper-weights or large pebbles. Although he had retired long ago from being the managing landlord of many of the houses which he had built in Birmingham and Smethwick and despite the fact that my uncle Wilfrid, the elder of his two sons, had taken over the running of the office at 5 Waterworks Road, my grandfather could never really bear to let go of the business which he had built up from nothing since he was twenty.

The original bay window at the far end was up a shallow step. A potted aspidistra stood on a whatnot in front of the window and Joey the canary's cage hung from a hook in the ceiling. The curtains closed along the line of the step, leaving Joey and the raised part in the dark at night.

The drawing room, to the left of the hall, had two casement windows which looked southwards towards the sundial, the row of pine trees and the distant tennis lawn. An upright piano stood between these windows. (All of the young Turners had had piano lessons.) Shelves on the opposite wall housed various curios which my grandfather had acquired on his considerable foreign travels. There were some none-too-comfortable armchairs, a settee and probably a small table or two. A door at the far end, to the right of the fireplace, led into the conservatory, which had its own heating furnace and chimney stack. Behind the conservatory were a wash-place and WC which had been added by Mr Chesshire in 1890. The hemispherical tip-up basin was set in a white marble counter. The WC pedestal was lavishly decorated with dark red flowers.

Next to the dining room was a smaller room, originally known as 'the study', which became my grandfather's bedroom when he could no longer get up and

1. The Lodge

down the stairs. As well as his bed it contained shelves full of books, including the *Encyclopaedia Britannica* in over twenty volumes. The telephone was attached to the hall wall just outside this room.

Beyond the baize-covered door, on the right, was the kitchen, which doubled as a sitting-room for the housekeeper and the maid. It had a kitchen range along its left-hand wall. I remember that it also had a cupboard, a large table and two armchairs. This was the last room in the main three-storey part of the building. A door next to it led into the scullery, a fairly large single-storey annexe with a quarry-tiled floor. Two parallel rows of skylights ran from north to south in its high ceiling. The cooking was done in there on a gas stove, though I realise that there must originally have been a fireplace, as the earliest photo shows a tall chimney stack to the scullery. There was a rather smelly yellow earthenware sink, supplied with cold water only, next to the door which led out into the back yard. The sink was in front of the only window.

Opposite the kitchen there was a passage across to the west side of the house. Leading off this there were two pantries and a staircase (under the front staircase) down to large cellars below the dining room, the hall and the drawing room. There was also a back staircase which went all the way up to the attic.

Between the scullery and the boundary wall with the Farm there was a narrow single-storey wing. A short roofed passage which ran through it from side to side, leading from the back yard to the side lawn, was known to us children as 'the tunnel'. It had wonderful amplifying acoustics, so we used to stamp our feet on its concrete floor on our way through. Beyond it there were two outside WCs. The nearer one opened onto the back yard and was evidently meant for the domestics. The other one opened onto the path round the side lawn and was used by the gardener.

On the first floor the master bedroom, my grandparents' room, was over the drawing room. Leading off it near its far right-hand end and down a few steps was a room, fifteen feet square, above the wash-place and WC behind the conservatory. My grandmother stored apples in this room, so it always smelt of them. There were three or four other bedrooms, each of which must also have contained a wash-stand complete with marble top, tiled back, jug and basin, soap dish, toothbrush holder and slop bucket. There would also have been a chamber-pot. The bathroom was on the first floor, next to the WC. The boxed-in bath had a shower over it. The WC had a step up to a mahogany bench seat which ran from wall to wall. This had a hinged middle section which revealed the pan when lifted.

Off the back staircase, half-way between the first floor and the attic, there was a little store-room with a window, which fascinated me. It had shelves full of old books including some children's story-books dating from the young Turners' childhood.

The only room in the attic which I remember was the large corner one above the dining room. My grandfather must have had the gable built onto it, as this is not shown on the earliest photo of the eastern side of the Lodge. There was already a skylight on the opposite side of the room. I never asked my mother who had had which room when the whole family lived there, but I think this one had belonged to one of my uncles. Through the gable window you could see the distant Waterworks chimney in Waterworks Road on the horizon.

The attic room on the front of the house above the master bedroom had a dormer window which must have been added by my grandfather, as it is not shown on the early photos. I remember that there was a similar dormer window above the middle windows on the eastern side of the house, but I have no photo which shows it. The maid and the housekeeper slept in these two rooms.

The attics.

During my early childhood the Turner household consisted of my grandparents James and Emily, my uncles Wilfrid, who married and moved to 131 Rotton Park Road in 1925, and Ralph, who went into lodgings some time

Above: The southern and eastern sides before the gable was added.

Right: The eastern side, showing the gable added by my grandfather, the tall chimney has been demolished. This photo also confirms my belief that the conservatory was not part of the original build but was added later by the Chesshires.

Left: Wilfrid outside a snowy Lodge, 1920s.

One man and his dog, James Turner outside the Lodge, 1928.

1. The Lodge

during the 1920s but was quite often at the Lodge (he did not marry until 1933) and also at week-ends and during school holidays my aunt Daisy, who was a teacher working in Wolverhampton. She used to drive home in her own car on Friday afternoons, at a time when relatively few women could drive and even fewer of them actually owned a car. Her bedroom was the one above the kitchen. She married and went to live in Moseley in 1928. When my grandparents became infirm during the 1920s, Miss Ethel Hughes became their resident nurse-companion and stayed until shortly after my grandfather's death. The domestic staff consisted of a housekeeper (Miss Harriet Pitchford, followed by Mrs Dutton) and a maid. I remember occasionally sleeping at the Lodge myself if my parents were away.

Also resident were Jack, Grandpa's very intelligent mongrel who had come from the Dogs' Home (some cruel former owner had docked his tail right off!), a large black cat called Judy and Joey the canary, who sang beautifully, always the same sequence of trills, in his cage in the dining room. Nobody ever took Jack for walks, but as the drive had no gate he used to go out on his own and was often to be seen trotting around the neighbourhood.

All six of my aunts and uncles got married but none of them moved very far away. The tennis lawn in front of the house was well used during summer week-ends. My father and sister played tennis too and I began to learn at school when I was nine. I also remember one very cold winter's day in 1924 or 1925 when I helped various relatives to make a big snowman on that lawn.

My grandparents were both round about seventy when I was born, so to me the word 'grandparents' means infirm, white-haired old people who rarely left their own house and garden and did nothing much, though my grandmother was skilled at embroidery and crochet. Grandpa, however, did teach me how to play draughts and I used to go across the garden sometimes in the evenings for a game with him. His seven grandchildren were also required by him to learn various party tricks, such as reciting the alphabet backwards as a verse*. My cousin Paul Beckett told me that whenever he did this correctly on one of his visits, he could rely on getting a shilling tip.

* Z Y X and W V
  U T S and R Q P
  O N M and L K J
  I H G feD cbA

Chapter 2

THE GARDEN

The Lodge's plot of land, with an area of 6,528 square yards or 1.13 acres and frontages of 90 yards 2 feet to Rotton Park Road and 72 yards to Wheatsheaf Road (the dimensions given in Chesshire, Gibson & Co's 1934 sale catalogue) must then have been the largest one belonging to any house on the Rotton Park estate. It was on a hill top, but this was not quite the highest point in Rotton Park (which is near the top end of City Road). It was bounded by Rotton Park Road to the west, the Farm to the north, Wheatsheaf Road to the east and the garage and garden of 22 Wheatsheaf Road, the Portland Lawn Tennis Club and our garden and house to the south. The eastern strip along Wheatsheaf Road, formerly a meadow (Mr Chesshire had owned a few horses and cows), sloping down to Wheatsheaf Road and had by my time been made into allotments. These, let to local gardeners, were out of bounds to the family, although only a slope down, with no fence or wall, separated them from the path along the top of the side lawn. They were probably set up during World War I, as May Nicholds of the Farm said in a tape-recorded interview that at that time every available piece of land in Rotton Park was used to grow food.

    The Lodge's original drive had been a long one, leading southwards parallel to the road from near the dining-room. Beyond the garden it ran part-way through a field then turned westwards to meet the road. Though no longer in use, it survived until shortly after the field was bought at an auction in 1906 by my grandfather and it is shown on many of the old maps. The narrow path leading from the Lodge past the eastern end of the tennis lawn to the bottom of our garden in my time was on part of the original line of this wider drive. I remember a large bush of very fragrant pink roses by the side of it, which survived and was later to be found in the garden of the house 141, where an acquaintance of mine, Mrs Betty Thurman, lived. When I visited her, many years ago the bush was still there, but I was disappointed to find that its roses were no longer fragrant.

The shortened drive, looking towards the Lodge.

The shortened drive, which was where the semi-detached house appropriately numbered 143 now stands, must have been created for my grandfather in or soon after 1905, as the Dockers had left in 1902 and it is not shown on the 1904 Ordnance Survey map. It was at right angles to the road, immediately south of the kitchen garden, from which it was separated by a fence and a bank with bushes and flower beds. A low ridge ran across the grassy part of the garden from a point near where the drive divided to the end of the tennis lawn, near the row of pine trees. We used to take running jumps off it. The earliest photo of the Lodge shows a fence next to this ridge.

Along the border with Rotton Park Road, south of the drive, there was a fence of iron hurdles with a hawthorn hedge on top of the bank behind it (the garden was a couple of feet higher than the road's footpath). This ran to where the front garden wall of our house began. I remember being fascinated as a child when some men came to lay the hedge. There was a small rarely-cut hayfield with plenty of buttercups, daisies, clover, yarrow and other wild flowers, bounded by the hedge, the flower beds and lawn near the drive, the western end of the tennis lawn and the northern wall of our house. The

Above: The row of pines in front of the Lodge.

Below: ...and towards Rotton Park Road.

Lodge and its garden were older than the game of Lawn Tennis, so what we knew as the tennis lawn may have originally been used by the Chesshires for croquet.

Our old photo albums show various family members in different parts of the garden. I have chosen from them the photos which show the garden best. However, nobody ever seems to have taken any photos of the kitchen garden. This was oblong, on the highest part of the land, next to Rotton Park Road and the Farm, from each of which it was separated by a brick wall six or seven feet high. On its eastern side, nearest to the Lodge, there was a triangular thicket of trees and bushes next to the curved part of the drive which went round the conservatory. The footpath to the kitchen garden led uphill from the back yard through this thicket. Some of these trees still survive in the gardens of the houses built in Rotton Park Road in 1934.

A heated greenhouse, containing a vine, stood on the northern side, next to the Farm. The garden's beds for fruit and vegetables were bordered by dark blue tiles each with one scalloped edge, set upright so that the decorative edges stood an inch or two above the ground. There were several apple trees. Many kinds of fruit (I particularly remember the luscious loganberries), vegetables and some flowers meant for cutting, such as sweet peas, were grown. In summer there were always cabbage white butterflies fluttering around and caterpillars chewing holes in the cabbages. By permission of her parents, my mother kept half a dozen hens in the north-western corner, where the house 153 and its front garden are now.

There was a boundary wall about four feet high, built of grey Black Country slag, separating the Lodge's garden and the allotments from Wheatsheaf Road, with a privet hedge just behind and above it. The wall was there first and the road was cut next to

Kay in Rangers uniform on the lawn, looking westward towards Rotton Park Road. The narrow path behind her is part of the line of the original drive. Another path with some rustic steps went from just beyond the right-hand edge of the photo up to meet the path along the top of the side-lawn near her left elbow.

The author cycling on the path between the side lawn on the left of the photo and the allotments on the right.

2. The Garden

*Left: Early tennis on the side lawn (c1910). Daisy, Wilfrid (back view) and a friend.
Right: Anyone for tennis? Barrett Lambourne from 129 with Max and Margery, his sons Eric and Gordon and my father, taken by Kay (1926).*

it. At the wall's northern end there was a double gate, used by the allotment holders, to an otherwise rarely used and somewhat grassy back drive belonging jointly to the Lodge and the Farm. This drive, created in 1906 when Wheatsheaf Road was cut, was separated from the Lodge's side lawn by a high stockade fence of vertical logs with a gate in it, near the big beech tree known as 'Jacob'.

The southern boundary of the Lodge's garden was no longer straight. My grandfather had given a further strip of his own lawn, to the north of our house and garden, to my mother in 1920, when my father acquired his first car, so that a garage could be built onto our house. However, as my father always kept his car in the Lodge's coach house, my parents never had a garage built. The low fence separating our former back garden from our new strip remained in its original position, with no gates, but just a gap, at each end of it. The new strip was not physically separated off from the Lodge's land until 1934, when the Lodge and 135 were both sold, though it did by then bear several small apple trees which my parents had planted. The garage wing was eventually built onto 135 for the couple who bought our house, Mr and Mrs Hampton.

Kay on the drive by the conservatory, with the raised kitchen garden and distant gables.

The Lodge garden therefore extended a few yards farther to the south beyond the bottom of our garden and then ran along the northern boundary of the Portland Lawn Tennis Club. It was separated from the upper tennis court by a bed of lupins, a low wall and the Club's very tall wire-netting fence. It became narrower again where it adjoined the garden of 22 Wheatsheaf Road, the farthest north of the older houses on the west side of that road. Round about 1920, my grandfather must have sold a strip of land to the owner of 22 so that a garage could be built onto the side of his house with a widened garden behind it. When I began to study the garden's history I was unable at first to work out how the present grey wall between the drives, garages and probably the back gardens of this older house, 22, and those of number 24, a detached house built in 1934 on the south-eastern corner of the Lodge's land, appears to be part of the original boundary wall although it runs along the wrong east-to-west edge of that strip. I eventually noticed that it is not as tall as the boundary walls onto the footpath and is different in structure from them. The original wall must have been demolished and then rebuilt along the other edge of the strip soon after this was sold.

Although there were no oaks, elms or horse chestnuts in the garden, there was a good variety of other trees, some of which, I am glad to say, are still flourishing. I remember beeches, a lime, a sycamore, some red may trees just south of the side lawn, a row of pines, a cedar of Lebanon, a yew and a weeping ash. These must all have been planted in Mr Chesshire's time as they were mature trees by the 1920s. There was a huge beech tree, known to the Turners as 'Jacob', near the northern end of the side lawn. Jacob was taller, and must have been older, than the Lodge itself. There was a wrought-iron seat all round the trunk. My grandfather's

After my grandfather gave an extra strip of land and of the Lodge's garden for a garage there was no wall.

The pines in winter, 1920s.

gardener used to go up a ladder to fasten the chains of a swing to a convenient horizontal branch every summer, much to our delight. The swing was taken down in winter.

Two full-time gardeners, Mr Wood and then Mr Tremlett, were employed during my childhood. They must have had to work very hard, with so much lawn to be kept in trim with a hand-pushed mower. Mr Tremlett had some help during summer evenings and week-ends from a schoolboy. There were flower beds along both sides of the drive and close to both long edges of the side lawn, with a good variety of flowers.

My grandparents occasionally allowed a Saturday afternoon garden party to be held at the Lodge in aid of charity. I particularly remember one of these, for the Birmingham Medical Mission, as I was given some money by my mother and was encouraged to go and enjoy the stalls, competitions and tea.

Three of the five Turner daughters, Elsie, my mother Winnie and Dora, who had all got married in summer by 1911, held their wedding receptions in the garden, a marquee being erected on the side lawn each time. Mabel, the youngest daughter, married in January 1913, so the reception was held indoors and her wedding photo was taken in the conservatory. Daisy, the third daughter but the last one to marry, held her reception in the garden on 8 September 1928 and I, aged nine, was one of her two bridesmaids. Monica Cartwright, my blonde fellow-bridesmaid, was the daughter of a college friend of Daisy's. I remember our pale turquoise blue taffeta dresses trimmed with silver

The weeping ash, 'Jacob' the huge beech tree and other trees around the Lodge's side lawn.

The side-lawn on Daisy's wedding-day, 8 September 1928.

braid, gold bangles (presents from the bridegroom), headdresses of silvered leather leaves on wire frames and our baskets of pink rosebuds, but sadly I retain no memory at all of the service at Carrs Lane Congregational Church or of travelling there and back.

The last-ever gathering in the garden was in July 1933, nearly four months after my grandfather's death, when my parents celebrated their Silver Wedding with a big garden party on a gloriously sunny day.

Chapter 3

THE FARM

The old lodge was surrounded by fields and hedges or fences, though no gates to these are shown on the maps, after Rotton Park was 'disparked' in 1553. So was **the Farm**, which was built just north of it in the early 1770s. The two buildings appear side by side on the maps under the joint name of 'Rotton (or Rotten) Park Lodge' or just 'The Lodge'.

Until Mrs Noel sold part of her land for the Reservoir in 1825 these buildings were approachable from three directions. There was the lane whose southern part was approximately where Stanmore Road is now and whose northern part eventually became part of Rotton Park Road. This ran from present-day Hagley

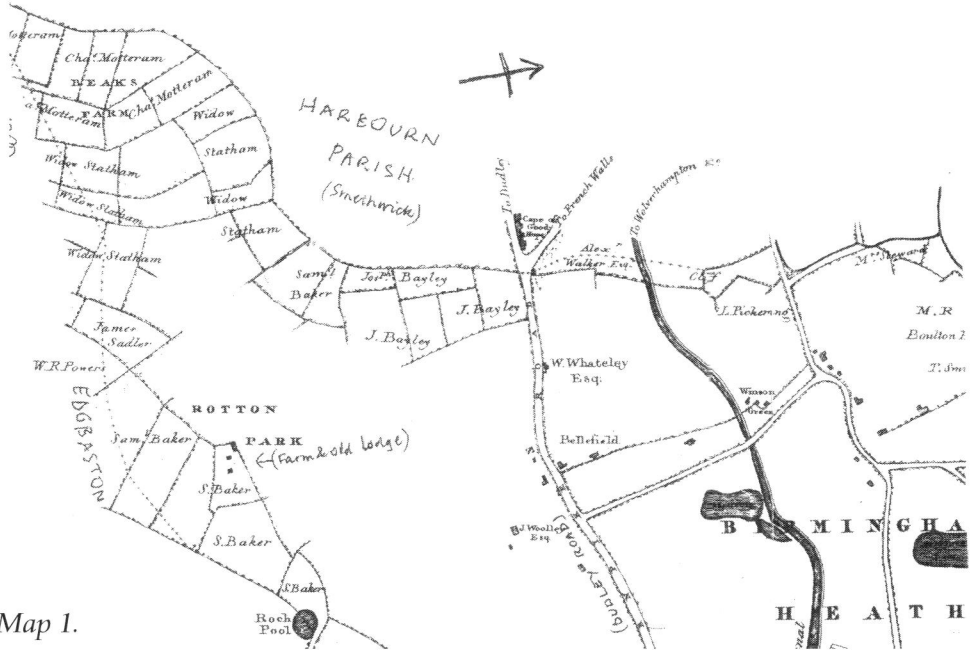

Map 1.

The earliest photo of the Farm, showing the lane on its northern side.

Road past the two buildings and on to present-day Dudley Road. But before the land for the Reservoir was sold it must also have been possible to reach the buildings, on foot or on horseback, from the end of the lane (shown on the Reservoir map in Chapter 6) which led northwards from the southern edge of the map to the medieval Roach Pool. This path on the Reservoir's site reached the Farm via the lane to the north of it. After the Reservoir filled up, this lane led only from Rotton Park Road to a nearby field. There is now a locked gate between 161 and 159 Rotton Park Road, across its end. Such a lane is shown on John Snape's 'Plan of the Parish of Birmingham' made in 1799. It ran along the border between two fields. The farm's inhabitants would have needed access to the only fish pond in the district.

The photos of the Farm, all taken after 1892, were lent by May Nicholds to my sister for copying. Copies were also made by the Birmingham Central Library and the Museum. They show the Lodge, not the old lodge, standing just south of the Farm.

After the Reservoir, which could originally be seen from the farmhouse, was constructed between 1825 and 1828, the Farm's land stretched as far as its grounds, to which the farmer had a private gate and a key. Pigs, cows, horses, chickens and possibly ducks were kept at the Farm (there was a circular pond near the corner of Gillott Road).

3. The Farm

The western side, showing the wing added by John Chesshire in 1890.

The farmyard, looking towards Rotton Park Road and Gillott Road.

Looking northwards from the lane towards Gillott Road.

Gillott Road (only a lane before the Railway was built) was widened by 1884. When Wheatsheaf Road and the curved part of Selwyn Road were cut, early in 1906, the Farm was left with only one field, north of the new back drive (shared with the Lodge) which was also created in that year. Five houses were built on this field in 1925.

I have found out from *Kelly's Directories* and the Censuses the names of some, though possibly not all, of the earlier nineteenth century farmers. **Samuel Baker** lived there in 1810. The many fields which he farmed seem to have covered much of what later became the Reservoir, as I know from **Map 1**, which is part of John Kempson's 1810 map of a walk round the boundaries of Birmingham. This map shows that Mr Baker also had the field across which the Reservoir's earth dam was later built, between the Roach Pool and the inverted U-shaped 'Rotton Park Turn' on the original (contour) Birmingham Canal. There may have been another farmer after him and before **James Ray**, who was there in 1878. He was succeeded by **Joseph Kinder** in 1883 and by **James Williams** in 1890. **Thomas Pritchett** lived in the nearby old lodge in 1845 and probably stayed there until it was demolished by John Chesshire soon after the sale of Rotton Park to Joseph Gillott in 1851.

Mr Gillott had wanted to pull the Farm down, as a building unworthy to be on his estate, but he never did so, probably because it was inhabited and there was no other building into which he could move the residents.

3. The Farm

After **Isaac Charles Nicholds** became Bailiff to the Rotton Park estate in 1892 and came to live at the Farm with his wife **Mary**, it became known as 'The Bailiff's Cottage', but to us it was always 'the Farm'. Nicholds is an unusual surname and all of the directories misspelt it as Nicholls.

There was, however, another farm, called **Rotton Park Farm**, on what is now George Dixon International School's playing field, near the present corner of City Road and Fountain Road. In 1871, the elderly farmer living there was **John Kite**. Before City Road was cut this farm could be approached only from Stanmore Road or from the lane which preceded it. Yet another farm, **Birmingham Heath Farm**, was at the western corner of present-day City Road and Dudley Road. In 1845 the farmer living there was **John Fawdry**. It was a large farm and most of its land was sold later to Mitchells & Butlers for their Cape Hill Brewery.

By my time the L-shaped farmhouse with small front and back gardens, the farmyard itself and some of the outhouses on the southern side of it were all that remained of the original buildings. They were separated from the road by a high brick wall with a slatted double gate. The cowsheds and pigsties on the northern side of the farmyard and the housing for the cart and the stable on the southern side of it had been demolished by about 1920, according to my late friend

The Farm, as it was in the late 1920s. The stable and the housing for the cart had been demolished.

Dorothy Hardie, née Lockie, who knew the Nicholds family and the Farm much better than I did.

The open lane alongside the northern border of the Farm led only a short distance to a field in Mr Nicholds' time. According to old maps which I have consulted, the rest of the lane had disappeared by 1906. But before the Reservoir was created in the 1820s it must have continued across the Reservoir's site as far as the Roach Pool.

The farmhouse and its yard were eventually hemmed in by houses, gardens, roads and the two drives, one leading to Rotton Park Road and the other to Wheatsheaf Road. No deeds about the Farm's area survive. The solicitor who had dealt with some changes to the area had destroyed them as they were over 25 years old and nobody seemed to want them.

I often had to walk past the Farm on my way to the railway station or to post letters in the pillar box at the corner of Gillott Road, so I knew from looking through the slatted gates what the farmyard and the front of the farmhouse looked like. On one occasion in the late 1920s I was sent by my mother to buy some eggs from Mrs Nicholds at the farmhouse door but I was not invited in, so to my regret I never saw the interior. Dorothy told me that there were two rooms downstairs. The front door led into a fairly large living-room-cum-kitchen. At the back, at right angles to it, there was a rarely-used 'best parlour'. She never went upstairs so she did not know how

The Farm, before 1924.

3. The Farm

many bedrooms there were. Sanitary arrangements, she said, consisted of a very smelly outdoor privy! The front garden had a hedge round it and some bushes and flowers. The back garden, containing mainly gooseberry bushes, was adjacent to the best parlour and also to the Lodge's coach house.

The late Brian Headley of 38 Wheatsheaf Road told me that his father who lived in Smethwick was once a postman working in Rotton Park, but he did not say when this was. His father would cycle to an office in Broad Street to pick up the post, then ride to the Farm, leave his bicycle there and deliver the letters on foot. (The Lodge's huge beech tree 'Jacob' ended up in Brian's garden, but as nothing would grow under it, he and a friend cut it down.)

The reduced-area Farm had been offered for sale as a building site in the auction held in 1911, with the fan-shaped plot behind it as a separate lot, but neither had reached its reserve price, so both remained unsold. The Nicholds family continued to live at the Farm until Mr Nicholds retired in 1930. He had hoped to be able to buy it and stay on, but this proved to be impossible, so he, his wife and May moved to 110 Gillott Road.

When the Farm was demolished in 1931 it was over 200 years old. A detached house, 155 Rotton Park Road, and a pair of semis, 157 and 159, all with garages, were built on its site by Stanton Marsh in 1932. Until a few years ago 159 was the surgery for a doctor who lived at 157.

The Farm being demolished in 1930.

Chapter 4

THE REMINISCENCES OF MISS MAY NICHOLDS

May Nicholds was born on 14 October 1893, lived to be 94 and retained her excellent memory to the end of her life. My parents, my sister and I all knew her. The information in this chapter comes from our own conversations with her, the transcript of a tape-recorded interview with her by Bob Willis of the Birmingham Museum and Art Gallery in 1986 and what Dorothy Hardie and her younger sister Dr Ruth Lockie, who had lived as children at 29 Wheatsheaf Road and had had May as their Nanny, told me.

  When Mrs Nicholds was on her deathbed she told May, who had always believed she had been born to Mrs Nicholds at the Farm, that she was actually her niece, not her daughter. May had been born to Mrs Nicholds' sister, but had come to the Farm as a baby and had been unofficially adopted by Mr and Mrs Nicholds as Julia May Nicholds and christened at Christ Church, Summerfield. (There was no legal adoption in England until 1927, after the Adoption Act had been passed in 1926.) She was correctly described in the 1901 Census as the niece of the householder. The three formed a happy and devoted family. Dorothy's snapshot of them shows a family likeness between May and Mrs Nicholds. May told Dorothy that after his wife's death Mr Nicholds had refused to discuss the matter of her adoption any further. She was never formally adopted.

  Isaac Charles Nicholds (Isaac to his family and Charlie to everyone else) and his wife Mary were both born in Packwood, between Birmingham and Coventry. He had come to Birmingham as a young married man to work in a factory, but his health had suffered and he had been advised by his doctor to seek an outdoor job. As Bailiff to the Rotton Park estate from 1892 until 1930, his main work was to keep all the hedges and fences round its many fields in good repair. He had an assistant, 'Old Tom', and a cart which was pulled by a shire horse called Captain. One sad day, some time before 1920, Captain dropped dead in a field where he

Isaac, May and Mary Nicholds, 1920s.

was working and Mr Nicholds had to bury him! Thereafter the two men had to push a handcart round the district. Mr Nicholds soon gave up putting up wooden fences where there were no hedges and used iron hurdles instead, because fences were promptly stolen for firewood, probably by people living in back-to-back houses in Icknield Port Road.

Several butchers, including Mr Izon with a shop in Dudley Road and Mr H. Walters at 167 Hagley Road, near The Ivy Bush pub, rented fields in Rotton Park in which to fatten cattle before slaughtering them.

James Loon, who had a dairy at 421 Dudley Road, opposite the end of Rotton Park Road, kept his cows in several rented fields and drove them along Rotton Park Road to be milked at the dairy and back to the fields, twice a day.

Gypsies, who were always around and often camped locally, would sometimes put their horses illegally into one of the fields at night. The Police were not allowed to enter the fields to turn them out onto the road, so Mr Nicholds had to do this. Policemen would then lead the horses away to the pound, which was next to The White Swan in Harborne Road and the Gypsies would have to pay to get them back.

May told me that she had spent a glorious childhood. Mrs Nicholds kept hens, sold eggs at the farmhouse door and also kept rabbits. May had a pet rabbit of her

James Loon driving his cows back up Rotton Park Road after milking them.

own. She said that you could see as far as Quinton and Cape Hill from the farmhouse. The only two roads anywhere near the Farm were Rotton Park Road and Gillott Road. In the 1890s Gillott Road had more houses than Rotton Park Road did, but it still had a few fields.

When May, as a little girl, went out with Mrs Nicholds they would sometimes meet the Docker baby from the Lodge, her junior by nearly three years, as he was being pushed in his pram by his Nanny. Mrs Nicholds and the Nanny would stop to chat and compare notes on how the two children were developing. May was later proud of having met the future Sir Bernard Docker in their push-chair and pram days.

After the Dockers left in 1902, the Lodge remained empty for three years. May used to play with three little boys who had no garden and the four of them would run happily round the grounds of the deserted Lodge. The long drive, she said, had a row of white posts connected by chains on each side of it.

Before Wheatsheaf Road and the curved part of Selwyn Road were cut in 1906 she loved to walk across the fields to the Reservoir and let herself into its grounds through the farmer's private gate. She told me that a seaplane had once come down on the Reservoir. This was some years later when she was an adult.

4. The Reminiscences of Miss May Nicholds

Mr Nicholds used to grow grass for hay in a field in Gillott Road near the Reservoir. After hay-making he would drive the hay-cart, with May happily riding on top of it, back to the Farm, where he would build a stack. Later, he would sell the hay to Mr Loon the dairyman.

After Captain died the cart remained unused in an outhouse for some time. May used to go into this outhouse, sit in the driver's seat, hold some reins made of string and imagine she was driving the cart to exciting places all over the world. Dorothy told me that Captain's stable and the outhouse for the cart were both demolished by 1920, though they continued to be shown on some later local maps after that.

May went to Barford Road Board School until she was fourteen. As she walked down Gillott Road on her way there in the mornings, she would see a maid kneeling by each open front door and scrubbing the doorstep.

She was not allowed to try for a place at the new George Dixon Girls' Secondary School, as she rarely went to school in winter because of her frequent coughs and colds. (Nevertheless, she managed to live into her nineties.)

After leaving school she became an apprentice at a dress shop in Monument Road where she learnt dressmaking and millinery. She moved later to a similar shop in Dudley Road, but from the age of 25 she had to work mainly at home, because Mrs Nicholds had become a semi-invalid. As well as being Nanny to the two Lockie girls, May did dressmaking, general sewing and mending and occasionally went out to local houses to make curtains. She was well known in the neighbourhood.

She used to shop for the family on Dudley Road and would have to trudge back, uphill for much of the way, to the Farm, carrying heavy bags. Joseph Gillott, who had allowed no shops on his estate, was dead and gone well before her time, but she told me that she would have liked to be able to invite him to do a shopping trip for her, without using his horse-drawn landau. He might then, she thought, have reconsidered his ban on shops in Rotton Park.

During World War I, she said, every available bit of land in Rotton Park was used to grow food. The playing field between Gillott Road, Rotton Park Road and City Road belonging to Mitchells & Butlers became a cornfield. She mentioned on the tape some allotments in Wheatsheaf Road, but whether these were the ones on the Lodge's land or some others I am not sure.

After her arrival at the Farm she had only two addresses in all of her long life. 110 Gillott Road, into which the family moved in 1930, is half of one of several identical pairs of semis with gardens of graduated lengths backing onto the Reservoir's grounds. The house was two years younger than May herself.

Mrs Nicholds lived to be 75 and Mr Nicholds lived to be 85. May stayed on alone in the house after they died, still supporting herself by sewing and odd jobs.

During her final few years she paid a young Irishman who lived next door to do shopping and some chores for her. She remained a keen member of Christ Church, Summerfield, some of whose parishioners helped her when she eventually became housebound. Dorothy, Ruth and I went to her well-attended 94th birthday party at her home on 14 October 1987.

    She was taken ill and had to go into the City Hospital in January 1988. One day she asked Ruth to buy a big box of chocolates for her to give to the nurses who had been so kind to her. When Ruth arrived at the Hospital next day with the chocolates, she was told that May had died.

Chapter 5

THE EARLY HISTORY OF ROTTON PARK

Rotton Park is known to have existed as early as 1307 as a hunting park, probably a deer park (these were very fashionable in the Middle Ages). It belonged to the **de Bermingham** family, the Lords of the Manor of Birmingham, who lived close to where the Bull Ring is now and would have enjoyed eating venison occasionally.

The northern part of the park lay in Birmingham and the southern part in Edgbaston, which did not become part of Birmingham until 1838. There would probably have been a ditch and a fence surrounding the park to prevent the deer from escaping. The park was bounded approximately by present-day Hagley Road and Sandon Road to the south, 'The Bear' pub, Shireland Brook and Cape Hill to the west, Dudley Road and Spring Hill to the north and Ladywood Middleway and Monument Road to the east. It is interesting to note that Mitchells & Butlers, whose Cape Hill Brewery was built in 1879, closed in 2003 and demolished in 2005, chose the 'Deer's Leap' as their trade mark, after a brook of that name had been found on an old map of their site. However, I doubt whether Rotton Park ever had two large rocks with a deep chasm between them like the ones on their trade mark. 'Deer's Leap' and 'Shireland Brook' are different names for the same stream.

There is still a wild part called 'Deer's Leap Wood' on what used to be Mitchells & Butlers' land, behind some houses on the right-hand side of Portland Road beyond City Road. I have found a photo and a description of it on the Web. The photo, which shows trees and a small pool, suggests what the whole of Rotton Park may have looked like before 1553, when it was 'disparked' and made available for agriculture.

There was a simple lodge, inhabited during the Middle Ages by a keeper, on the high ground between the present-day Rotton Park Road and Wheatsheaf Road. It was an L-shaped building with one small outhouse, standing in an oblong plot.

Later, it may not have been continuously inhabited, but during some periods just used by the owners whenever they came to hunt. An early sixteenth-century park-keeper who did live there was **John Praty** or **Pratty**. (I found his name in a footnote in 'A Survey of Birmingham in the year 1533'.) It became a second farmhouse after Rotton Park was 'disparked'. According to Map 3, the 1845 Tithe Map, it was by then inhabited by **Thomas Pritchett**, who farmed five fields between present-day Rotton Park Road and the Reservoir. It was eventually the site of the house 'Rotton Park', later renamed 'Rotton Park Lodge', which was built in about 1852. 'The Farm', later also known as 'The Bailiff's Cottage', had been built next door to the old lodge in the early 1720s. On all except one of the old maps which I have examined, the two appear side by side under the joint name 'Rotton (or Rotten) Park Lodge' or just 'The Lodge' and are the only buildings in the area. The exception is Humphrey Sparry's 1718 Map of Edgbaston (not included in this book) which shows the old lodge just north of the Edgbaston and Birmingham boundary, but was made a few years too early to show the Farm as well.

A fish pool called Roach (or Roch) Pool had been created in Rotton Park during the Middle Ages by damming up three brooks, one of which was the Rotton Park Brook, in the valley south-east of the old lodge. A path led from the north side of the Farm past this pool to join a lane leading to what later became Monument Road. Roach Pool became the deepest part of the Reservoir after this was constructed between 1825 and 1828 by Thomas Telford. Part of the lane occasionally comes into view if the Reservoir is nearly empty (it was partially drained during World War II because the full Reservoir was too good a navigating aid for German bombers and it almost dried up during the drought year of 1976.)

My gardener, Neville Mattison, who knows the Reservoir well, tells me that after a dryish summer in 2016 the water level was fairly low in early autumn and the opportunity was taken to do some repairs.

The **de Bermingham** family fizzled out early in the sixteenth century. Unfortunately no documents about its decline survive. As a result, Rotton Park was forfeited to the Crown in 1536. It was held by **John Dudley** from 1545 until his execution in 1553 for his involvement in the Lady Jane Grey affair and it then reverted to the Crown. **Queen Mary** granted it to **Thomas Marrow** of Berkswell, Warwickshire, in 1553. His descendant **Sir Edward Marrow** sold the park to **Humphrey Perrott** of Belbroughton, Worcestershire, in 1630. Several generations of Perrotts owned the park and some of the owners sold off portions of land round its borders. Until **John Perrott** inherited Rotton Park in 1737 all of these owners had continued to live in Belbroughton and had visited Rotton Park only occasionally, but John chose to live in Rotton Park itself.

5. The Early History of Rotton Park

Perrott's Folly from the garden of Monument House.

5. The Early History of Rotton Park

He lived in the building later renamed 'Monument House' on the corner of Monument Road (formerly Monument Lane) and Waterworks Road and the northern tower 'Perrott's Folly' was built at the far end of his garden.

An article in *Edgbastonia* (a monthly magazine delivered free to all the best houses in Edgbaston) for January 1898, about a later dweller in the newer part of Monument House, **Alexander Herbert Bates**, makes it clear that the older part of that house was where John Perrott had lived. The article includes a drawing of the front of Monument House. The house was enlarged some time after John Perrott's death. I also found a photo of Perrott's Folly and the back of Monument House taken in 1893 in a book called 'Birmingham Faces and Places, Volume 5' in the Central Library.

Drawing of Monument House.

As his only son had died in infancy, John Perrott left Rotton Park to his daughter **Catherine** (1747-1828), who had married **Walter Noel** in 1764. However, she and her husband lived in Belbroughton, so Monument House had other tenants or owners until about 1899, when it was demolished and replaced by shops built by my grandfather. Its site is now occupied by the Karis Medical Centre. The tower, **Perrott's Folly**, which has occasionally been open to the public, was disposed of in 2013 for an annual rent of one pound and is now part of an art gallery complex. I have climbed up it three times but got to the open top only on my first visit, when the tower was a weather observatory. On my later visits we were not allowed to go any higher than the top room.

I know of two locally-written books on the history of Rotton Park, copies of which may be found in libraries. These are '**Rotton Park – A History**' by **L.G. While** (1980), printed privately and '**Rotton Park and Round About**', a monograph by **John Morris Jones** (also 1980). All of the monographs about various parts of Birmingham which Mr Jones, a former Headmaster of George Dixon Junior School, wrote for schoolchildren are now available on the Web, at ***www.bgfl.org/johnmorrisjones***. He gives some **mis**information about the Lodge and the Farm (I wish I had known him!) but there is much which is of interest and his maps are good.

Left: Perrott's Folly.

Chapter 6

MAP 2, THE 1825 RESERVOIR MAP

During my University of Birmingham studies I acquired from Peter Leather a photocopy, made from his own photocopy, of a 26-inch by 40-inch map of the land purchased in 1825 by the Birmingham Canal Company for the construction of Rotton Park Reservoir (later renamed Edgbaston Reservoir) by the engineer **Thomas Telford** (1757-1834). The map, the original of which is in the Waterways Archive in Gloucester, shows the Farm and the old lodge near its top left-hand corner, under the joint name of 'The Lodge' and also the 'New road' to be cut, *i.e.,* Rotton Park Road. I think it is unlikely that this map has ever appeared in any previous book about Birmingham. Permission has been granted by the Waterways Trust for my version of it to be printed.

I made this by going over every line and every letter on a reduced photocopy with a fine black pen. Some distortion near the left-hand and lower edges of the map had occurred during the photocopying and reduction, so I cut slices which showed no details in which I was interested off these, thus leaving the wording still legible when the map was reduced again. Apart from the areas and boundaries of the four owners' parts of the Reservoir's site, the map shows few details of hedges or paths, as most of the land would finish up under water. We are also left guessing where Mrs Noel's oak trees were.

Although the note near the bottom left-hand corner states that the land purchased from its four former owners is coloured blue, green, pink and yellow, my large photocopy is, of course, in black and white only. I am grateful to Ms Caroline Jones, Archive Research Assistant at the Waterways Trust, for looking out the original map, colouring a copy of my version in accordance with it and returning this to me. The four colours have now been represented by different kinds of shading.

By far the largest area (57 acres) of the land for the Reservoir was purchased from **Mrs Catherine Noel** for £10,000. Although it consisted mainly of fields separated by hedges, it also had some oak trees which had to be cut down in the correct season for tree-felling. The wood was sold on Mrs Noel's behalf by her agent.

6. Map 2, the 1825 Reservoir Map

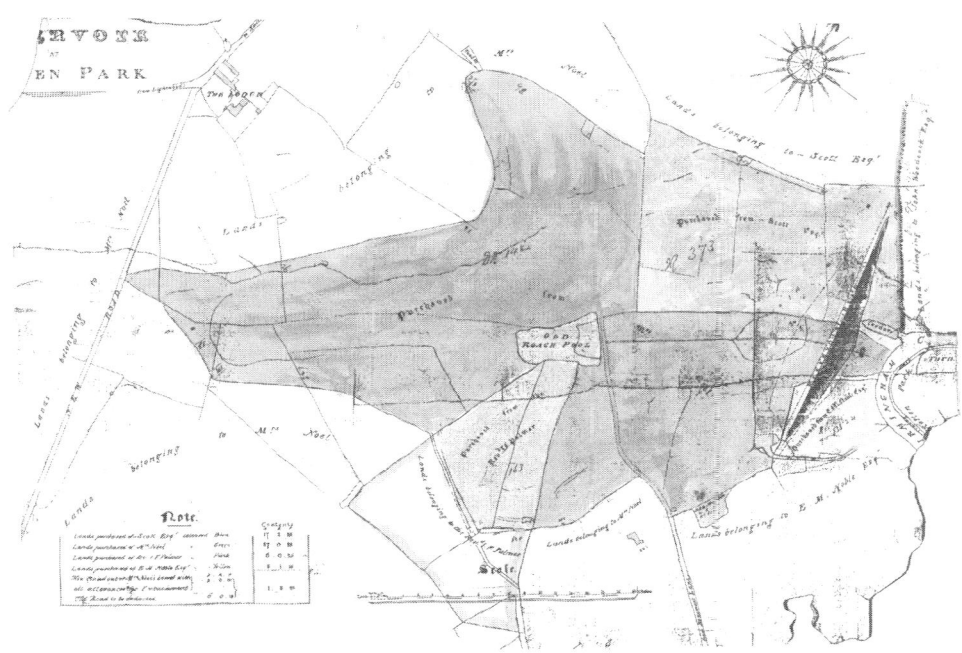

Map 2. The larger part of document reference BW165/28/1/5/1, The Waterways Archive, Gloucester, showing the land purchased in 1825 by the Birmingham Canal Company for the construction of Rotton Park (later Edgbaston) Reservoir. Reduced by the author, 2009. Size of original map 2658 x 959mm.

Her solicitor in Stourbridge, Mr Henry Roberts, had sent a letter (hand-written, of course) to the solicitor Mr Lee, the Chairman of the Birmingham Canal Company, saying that as Mrs Noel had raised no objection to selling the land, he hoped that the Company would be willing to make a new road for her, so that she would still be able to get from side to side of her remaining land when the middle part of it had disappeared under water. This they agreed to do. I found his letter and Mr Lee's reply in the Archives section of Birmingham's former Central Library.

Rotton Park Road (formerly Lane) was therefore cut across Mrs Noel's land. It met the old lane to Birmingham Heath (now Dudley Road), which became its northern part, near the Farm and the old lodge. That is why there is a slight bend at this junction.

According to John Morris Jones, the lane had been up-graded to the status of a suburban street by 1872. I can remember, as a child in the 1920s, seeing a lamplighter walking along the road in the evenings and turning the gas lamp-posts on with a hook on the end of a pole. The road now has powerful overhead electric lighting.

Mrs Noel died in 1828, so she may never have seen or used her new road.

Aerial view of the Reservoir taken by David Wilkins.

Chapter 7

JOSEPH GILLOTT'S 1851 PURCHASE OF ROTTON PARK

Joseph Gillott bought Rotton Park from **Charles Noel**, Mrs Catherine Noel's grandson, in 1851, reputedly paying just under £100,000 for the 500 acres. Gillott, born in Sheffield in 1799 and trained as a cutler, had arrived in Birmingham as a penniless youth. After working for a period in the 'toy' (steel button and buckle) trade he had made a fortune by mechanising and improving the production of steel pen-nibs. ('Joseph Gillott was a bad man who made men steel pens and told them they did write', as an old saying goes.) By the mid 1800s he was a rich man living in Westbourne Road, Edgbaston, with his wife and their large family which included an invalid son. He collected valuable old violins, including several made by Stradivari, and paintings, some of them by his personal friends William Etty and J.M.W.Turner. He had also acquired a coat of arms incorporating a wheatsheaf, which accounts for the name of Wheatsheaf Road.

Joseph Gillott.

Before finalising the purchase of Rotton Park he had climbed to the top of Perrott's Folly but had descended its spiral staircase rather more quickly than he had gone up it when he had felt the tower rocking slightly in a high wind. (I found this nice story in Showell's 1885 *'History of Birmingham'*.)

He founded **The Gillott Trust** and intended to lay Rotton Park out as an upper middle-class residential district and to sell off sites for houses until the whole estate was resold, chiefly for the financial benefit of his grandchildren. One of his daughters, **Maria Perks**, who had no children (she was nearly 40 when she married) took a poor view of this arrangement and sued the Trust over it in 1875, after which its affairs were taken over by the Court of Chancery. Joseph had decreed that there should be no shops or licensed premises in Rotton Park. He wanted to have the Farm pulled down as a building unworthy to be on his estate, but this was not done, possibly because there was no other house available into which the farmer who lived there could move. He created several new roads and named two of them after his sons **Montague** (who seems to have died young) and **Algernon**.

The land agent who acted for him in the purchase of Rotton Park was **John Chesshire**, who became both a personal friend and a Trustee. Mr Chesshire, married with three children and living in Vicarage Road, Edgbaston, seized the opportunity to buy for himself the old lodge, situated in over an acre of land just south of the Farm. It must have been he who had the building pulled down, as this is shown, together with the Farm, as 'THE LODGE' in the top left-hand corner of Map 2, the 1825 map of the land bought for the Reservoir. An unsigned obituary of Mr Chesshire in the free magazine *Edgbastonia* dated December 1894 says that his house was built 'on the site of an old farm'. He called this new house, which was probably built in 1852, simply 'Rotton Park'.

Joseph Gillott died in January 1873 (some books wrongly say 1872). The Harborne Branch railway opened in 1874. Gillott Road existed as a lane before the railway was built, but it was widened over a period and acquired many houses. It was, of course, named after him. Stanmore Road, which originally ran from Hagley Road only as far as Portland Road, was cut on the other side of the railway, replacing the field path which had led from the old lodge and the Farm to a point near the junction of Hagley and Sandon Roads. It owes its name to the fact that Mr Gillott had also owned a house called 'The Grove', with a beautiful garden, in Stanmore, Middlesex. He had bought this in 1853 as a second home conveniently near to London. Stanmore Road became a popular place to live because Hagley Road station was just round the corner, making it easy to get into town.

Some of the information about the Gillott family comes from a University essay (undated) by Di Bryan, entitled *'The Gillott Family and Rotton Park Estate'* which I found in the Library at Winterbourne some years ago.

Chapter 8

MAPS 3 TO 8 AND MAP 10

These maps show developments in Rotton Park over about sixty years, in date order. All of them except Map 8 are ones which I found in the Archives and Heritage Department of the former Birmingham Central Library. They were photocopied and are reproduced by kind permission of the then Head of that Department, Patrick Baird. (To fit legible versions into a book of this size, some of them have had to have slices cut off their edges.)

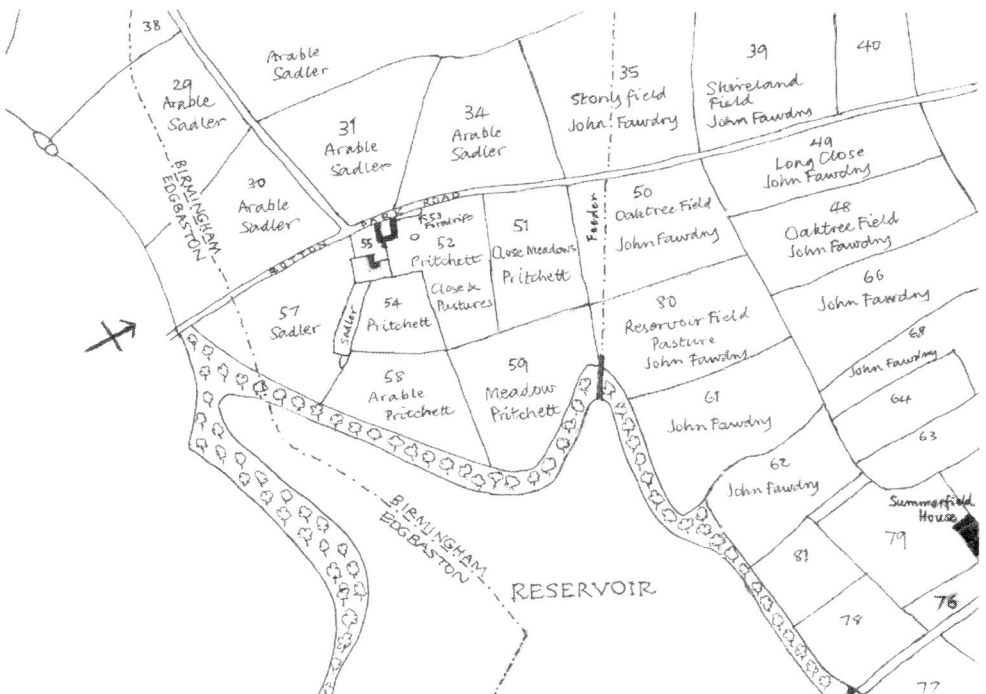

Map 3: From Tithe Map of St. Thomas & All Saints Parishes, Birmingham 1845.

Map 3, which I copied from part of an 1845 tithe map, shows the Reservoir and the southern part of Rotton Park Lane or Road. The Farm and the old lodge are the only buildings in the area. There are numbers, but no farmers' names, on the fields on the original map, but I found out who had farmed which fields from another map.

Map 4 is a map which was presented to Birmingham Central Library some years ago. Its origin is not known for certain, but Richard Albutt, a map expert at the Library, told me that it was probably created in about 1850 for Mrs Noel's grandson Charles Noel of Belbroughton when he decided to sell Rotton Park. If this is so, he seems to have thought that nobody would want to buy the whole area, so he had divided it up into districts labelled 'FIRSTLY', 'SECONDLY', and so on. However, Joseph Gillott did want to buy all 500 acres of Rotton Park. The map shows the Farm with the old lodge to the south of it.

Map 5 (1887) is by William Blood. Hagley Road has by now acquired some houses.

Map 6 (1890) is pieced together from four sheets of the 1:500 Ordnance Survey maps which happen to converge at Monument House. It shows the house,

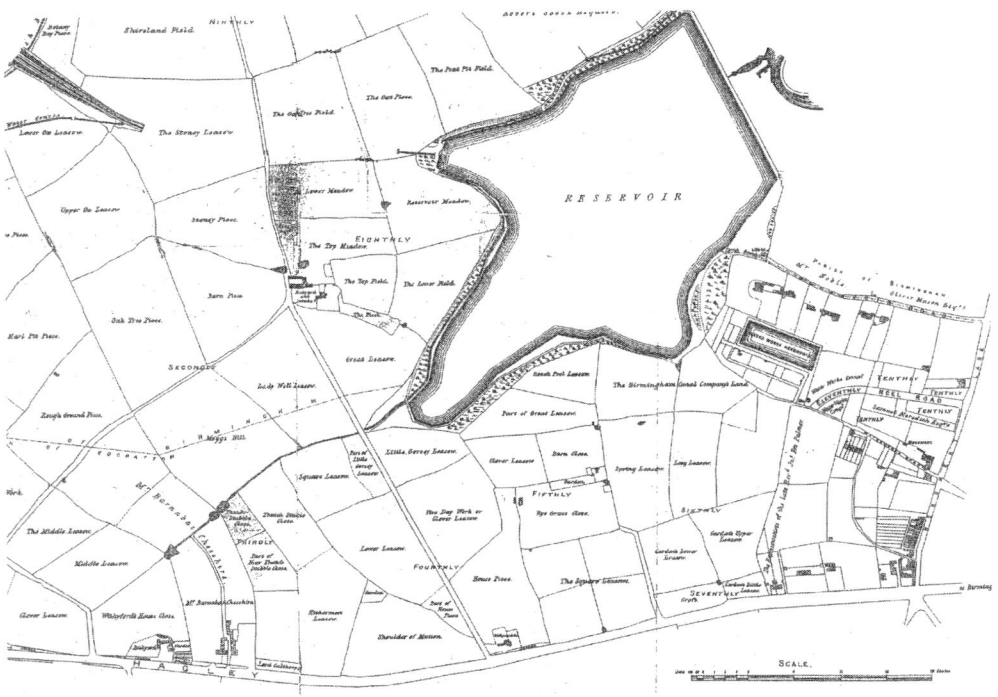

Map 4: Rotton Park, c.1850. Origin unknown but connected with the forthcoming sale.

8. Maps 3 to 8 and Map 10

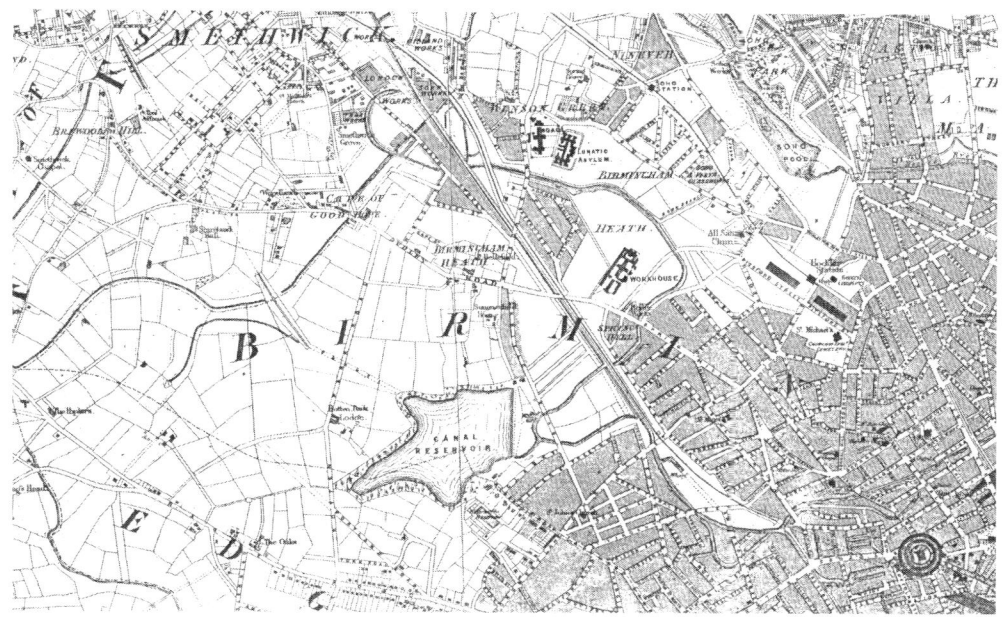

Map 5: Birmingham and its environs 1857.

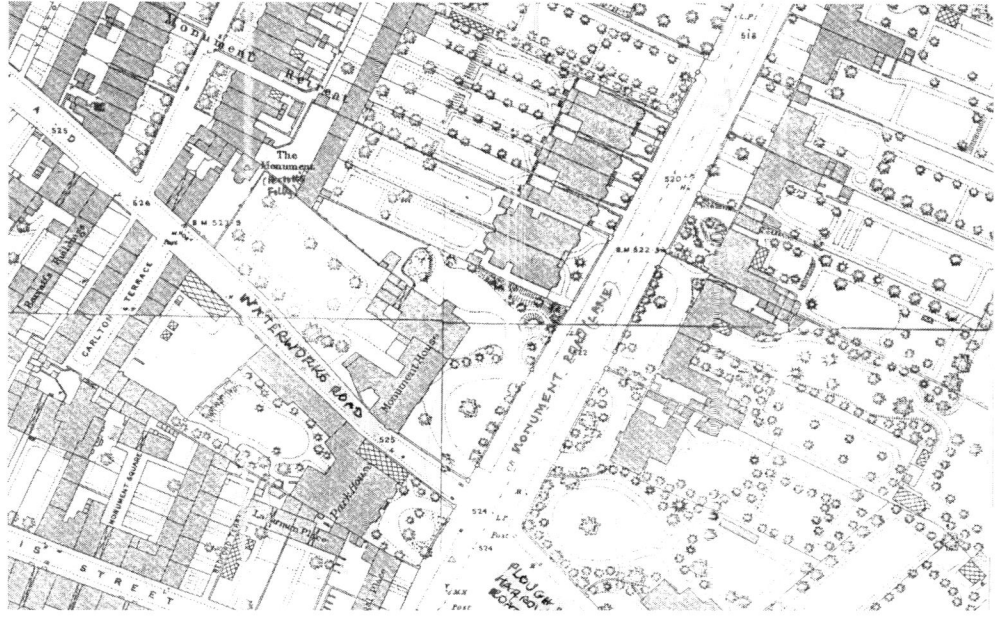

Map 6: Parts of four Ordnance Survey Maps, scale 1/500, surveyed in 1890.

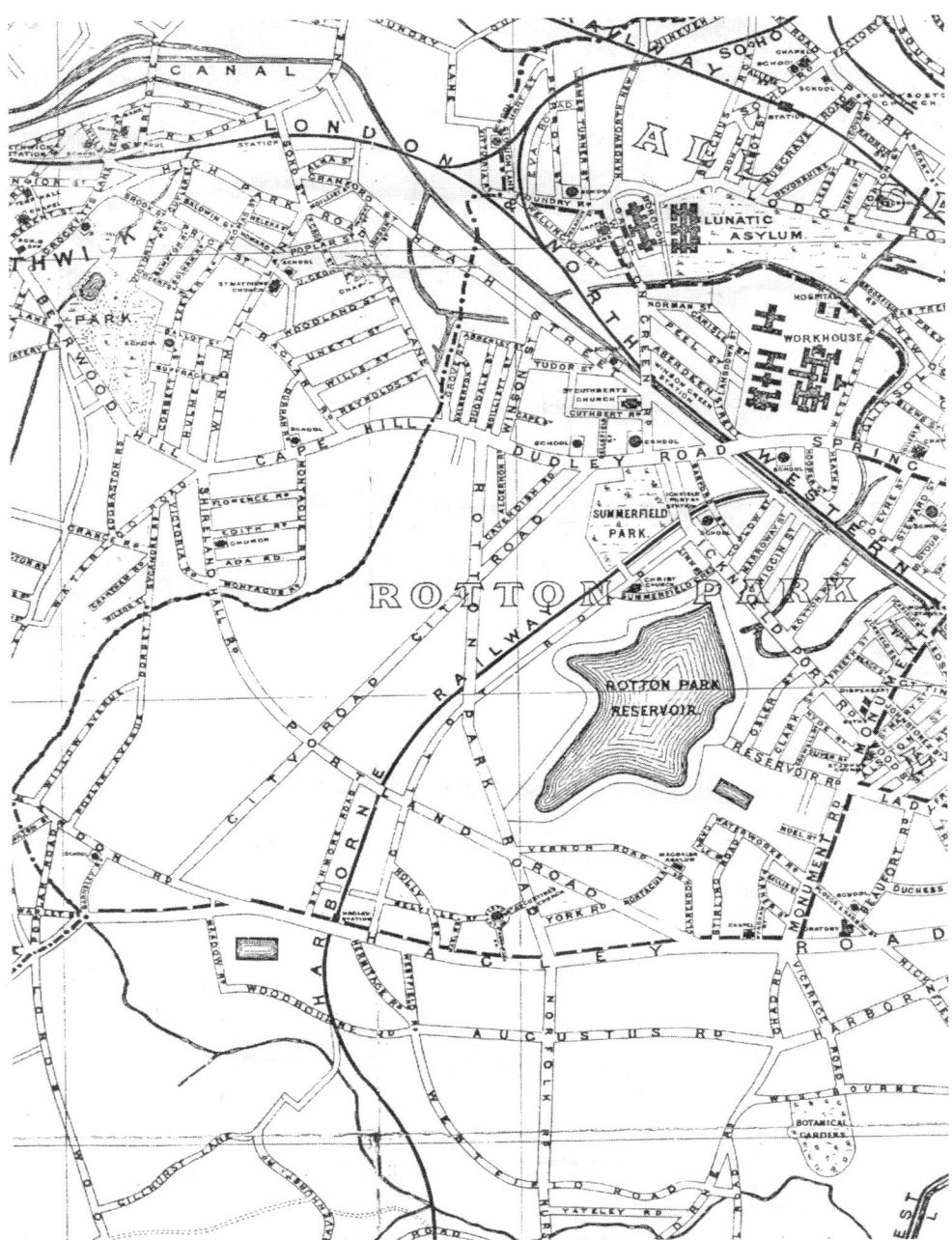

Map 7: Part of a map of Greater Birmingham published in 1894 by The Midland Educational Company Limited.

8. Maps 3 to 8 and Map 10

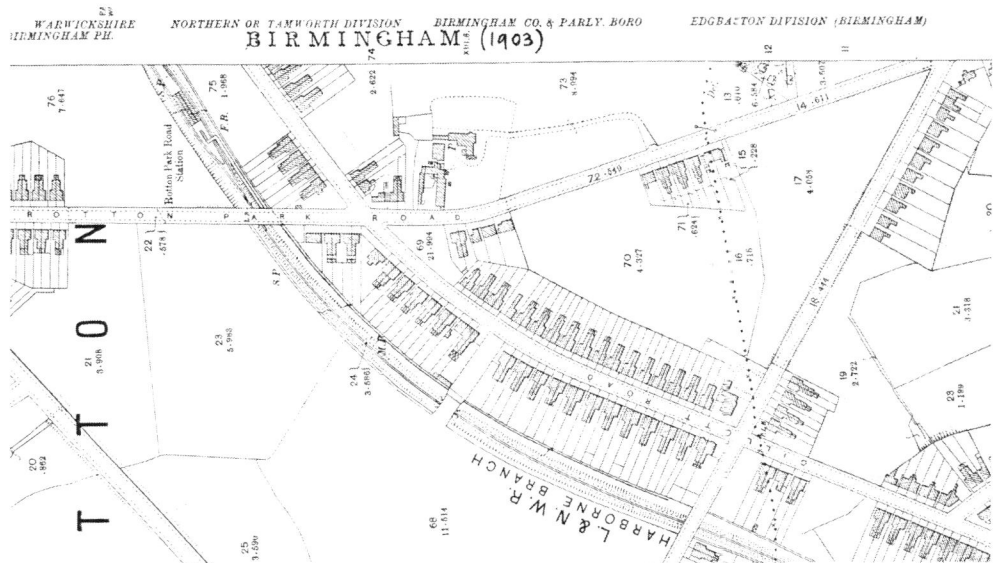

Map 8: Enlarged from Old Ordnance Survey Map, Bearwood 1903.

its garden and the Monument (Perrott's Folly), as well as James Turner's office building next door to it and part of Monument Retreat, two terraces with a total of 28 houses, which he had built.

Map 7 (1894) shows the development of new roads, but few buildings. Summerfield Park has only one bridge over the railway leading to it from Gillott Road. The second bridge must have been built later, when the Park was enlarged after the first part of Selwyn Road, from City Road to Gillott Road, was cut in 1898.

Map 8 (1903) is an enlarged part of an Ordnance Survey map reissued in 1986 by The Godfrey Edition and is reprinted by kind permission of Alan Godfrey.

Map 10 (1955) is a reduced part of an out-of-copyright 1:1250 Ordnance Survey map. It shows Tennis Courts where later maps show the Squash Club.

Roads which I remember being cut during my childhood are Wadhurst Road, Manor Road North, Mayland Road, Newnham Road, Hannafore Road and Jacey Road.

This last road, a cul-de-sac off Rotton Park Road almost opposite our house, was photographed from our front bedroom window by my sister, who mounted the photo in her album together with the date, so I am sure that it was cut in July 1929, though I have read in other books that it was cut in 'about 1930'. Although the field in which the new cul-de-sac was being cut was wide open to the road,

Map 10: Rotton Park 1955.

An excerpt from Kay's photo album.

there were still two horses in it. As you will also see from my sister's album page, the horses decided to cross the road early one morning to find out whether the grass was any greener in the Lodge's garden.

Jacey Road's name comes from the initials of Birmingham solicitor **Joseph Cohen (1889-1979)**, who had recently sold several cinemas of which he was a joint owner and had decided to invest the money in buying land and creating new roads. There is another Jacey Roads in the Birmingham area in Shirley.

I am grateful to Dr Anthony Joseph for information about Mr Cohen.

Chapter 9

MAP 9 AND THE 1911 SALE CATALOGUE

An auction of the remainder of the Gillott Estate was held on Thursday 15 June 1911. The Trustees had hoped to sell off all of the 24 lots and then to wind up the Trust. However, a paragraph in the *Birmingham Daily Post* for Friday 16 June 1911 says that only lots 3, 4, 5 and 7 had been sold, for £12,000, £1,180, £3,000 and £7,250 respectively, as none of the other lots, including the Farm (listed as a building site) had reached its reserve price.

The large sale catalogue and an even larger coloured map were given to my sister by May Nicholds. Both were subsequently reduced and photocopied in black and white for its own archives by Birmingham Central Library. The catalogue gives considerable details of each of the lots, most of them meadows being rented by farmers and butchers for the grazing and fattening of cattle, together with the names of the tenants or co-tenants and the rents currently being paid. These range from one pound ten shillings (£1.50) for a shared tenancy to about twenty pounds per annum. The minimum amounts to be spent on any houses to be built on the lots are stated. For semi-detached houses the lowest such amount was £150 per house, though most houses were to have at least £375 spent on them. The highest minimum, for a detached house to be built on Lot 10 in Hagley Road, was £750.

The original Gillott estate had extended as far north as Birmingham Heath (now Dudley Road), but the 1911 map stops at the corner of Rotton Park Road and City Road. The northern part of the estate from City Road to Dudley Road and the new roads running off that part of Rotton Park Road are shown on the 1903 Ordnance Survey map as being by then fully developed with terraces of houses and the back of City Road Junior School.

Rotton Park Road, Cavendish Road and Algernon Road are mentioned in the notice in the *Birmingham Post* of an auction of freehold building lands and

9. Map 9 and the 1911 Sale Catalogue

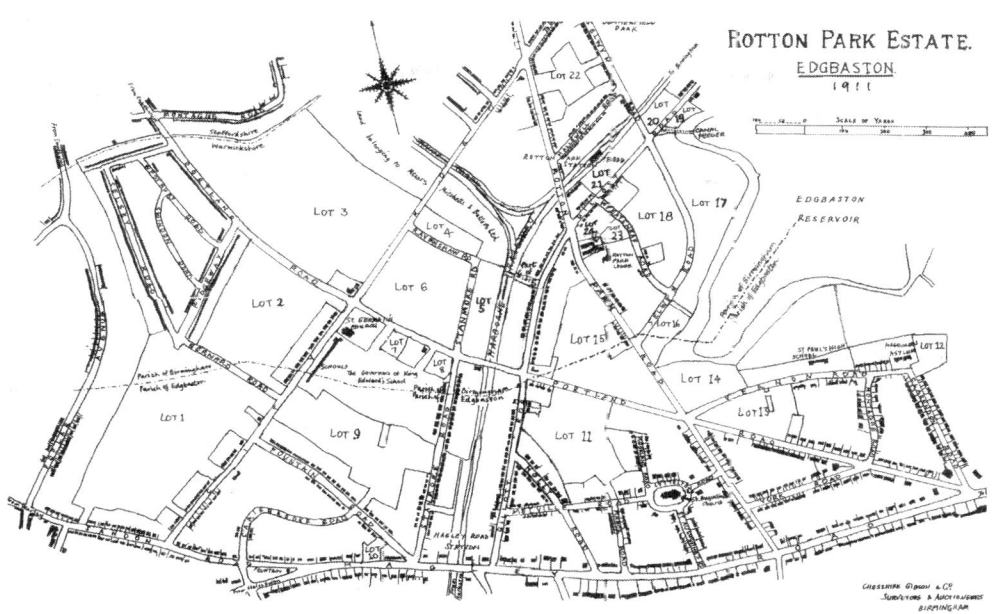

Map 9: Traced, reduced and slightly simplified by Margery Elliott, 2008, from the original map with the 1911 Sale Catalogue.

freehold residences in the King's Court of Justice by Mr Denston Gibson of Chesshire, Gibson & Co, to be held on Friday 29 July 1898. That part of the Gillott estate must have been sold off then. Knowing that Mr Gillott had decreed that there should be no shops on his estate, I had often wondered how there came to be a shop (a baker's called Jennings in the 1920s) on the corner of Rotton Park Road and Cavendish Road, but this sale explains why it had been able to exist. Its triangular site was probably unsuitable for a dwelling-house and garden.

The only time I remember going into that shop was when I was about ten years old. My mother ran out of bread one afternoon and sent me there with orders to buy 'whatever loaf they still have left'. I was actually sold a crusty white loaf which had just come out of the oven. It smelt wonderful and the temptation was too great. By the time I got home I had pulled off and eaten all of the top crust. Expecting a wigging, I was astonished when my normally stern mother merely said 'Well, I suppose we have all done that in our time'.

Here are some points of interest about the 1911 map, gleaned from the catalogue:

Lot 5 consisted of two plots of land, one on each side of the Harborne Branch railway (opened in 1874), which owned the bridge connecting them. This bridge and the strip of land connecting it to Gillott Road are shown on the 1903 Ordnance Survey map. Most of the lot lay to the north-west of the railway. I remember the field path which crossed this bridge with a wide gate onto Gillott Road, where the block of flats, number 323, now stands. There is still a narrow (locked) gate behind the flats onto the Walkway's land where the railway used to be.

Lot 9 in Fountain Road, opposite the end of Carisbrooke Road (which had been cut soon after 1900), had been intended to be developed as an extension of Carisbrooke Road with a right turn into Stanmore Road and already had the necessary sewers, but this extension was never made. A house was eventually built on the lot.

Lot 12 at the outer corner of Vernon Road and Clarendon Road included the Vernon Tennis Club, of which I have found only one other mention but no details.

The Fountain is shown near the eastern point of the triangle of land bounded by Hagley Road, Sandon Road and the top part of Meadow Road. This stood at what was the highest inhabited point of Birmingham (just over 600 feet above sea level) until Quinton and Kingstanding became parts of the city. According to Showell's 1885 *Dictionary of Birmingham*, an ornamental fountain had been built there 'recently'. My mother could remember it. Ornamental it may have been, but for reasons of hygiene there was no water visible. By my time it had been replaced by a simpler closed fountain, in which water was pumped up to the top of a tall metal pipe to give it a head and was then allowed to run down a concentric outer pipe. There was an empty basin round the outer pipe a few feet above its base and the whole structure was painted dark green, The water then ran through a pipe under Hagley Road into a reservoir (originally open, but later covered) which supplied water to the buildings in Hagley Road and Broad Street. This second fountain was demolished before 1933 (probably after the raised reservoir in Harborne Road, Warley, was constructed) and a nearby horse-trough went later. I wonder how many present-day inhabitants of Fountain Road know why their road has that name.

Chapter 10

THE CHESSHIRES

The portrait, signature and life-story of John Chesshire in this chapter come from an unsigned obituary in the free monthly magazine *Edgbastonia* for December 1894. This states that the photo, taken late in his life, gives little idea of what a tall and fine-looking man he had been in earlier years. The dates of birth of his offspring come from a legal document dictated and signed by his daughter Adelaide in 1903.

Information has also come from Geoff Chesshire of Cardiff, who, as a member of another branch of the Midland's Chesshire family with a common ancestor, has done considerable research on the whole family tree. We were put into touch by Geoff's cousin, the late Professor John Chesshire of the University of Sussex, whom I had contacted after finding his name on the Web, in the hope that he might be a direct descendant of the earlier John. (He was not, but he had heard of the Birmingham firm of Chesshire, Gibson & Co.) Geoff has recently discovered that the Birmingham John's second child and eldest son, who lived for only six months, was christened John Barnabas on 31 March 1842 and was interred on 19 September in the same year. Adelaide had mentioned him as just 'Barnabas' on her document without giving the actual dates of his birth and death.

'*All Saints' Church, Wribbenhall, 1879-2004*', a booklet issued in 2004 by Mrs Roz Mace, Churchwarden of that church near Bewdley, Worcestershire, has supplied facts about the three Chesshire vicars of the church, as has another pamphlet, *'Wribbenhall – The Day Before Yesterday'*, from which she sent me a few photocopied pages.

John Chesshire was born in Bath Street, Birmingham, on 1 May 1813, the eldest of a family of five sons and two daughters. His father, Barnabas (1774-1852), born in Knowle, had moved to Birmingham and had become a builder. During John's boyhood the family moved to a house in Temple Row with a builder's yard adjacent to it, on a site which is now part of the department store, The House of Fraser. By 1845 they had moved again to a house called 'The Oaks', with considerable land behind it, on the north side of Hagley Road. Holly Road and its houses and gardens now occupy its site.

Three of John's brothers, Barnabas junior, Edwin and Humphrey, became respectively a solicitor, a distinguished ophthalmic surgeon and a clergyman. John, however, who had been sent to Peterborough Cathedral School with a view to going on to University and then taking Holy Orders, had been fetched back home when he was thirteen, despite the fact that he was showing considerable academic promise. His father, who had become an auctioneer, surveyor and land agent by 1819, needed John's help in his business and eventually took him into partnership. Humphrey also worked with them for a time between leaving school and going to University.

Barnabas senior had retired by 1850. In that year, William Gibson of Edgbaston joined John as a partner and the firm changed its name from 'Chesshire and Son' to 'Chesshire, Gibson & Co'. William Gibson's son Denston joined his father and John as a partner in 1875. Other partners' names were occasionally added to or removed from the firm's name. The Chartered Surveyors' offices were at various times at 37 Temple Row, 11 Bennetts Hill and 98 New Street. After John's death the firm moved to 21 Waterloo Street and later to 63 Temple Row.

The only other Chesshire ever to join the firm was John's great-grandson, James Hugh Cecil Chesshire (1916-2000), a Chartered Surveyor who became a Major in the Royal Engineers during World War II and was awarded the Military Cross for his secret work in Albania. Taken prisoner and sent to Colditz Castle, he was eventually liberated by advancing American troops. He returned to the firm as a partner after the War and retired in 1981. Geoff tells me that James was later much involved in the development of Redditch as a new town.

Chesshire, Gibson & Co merged with the international firm DTZ Debenham Tie Leung in 1988. That firm's Birmingham office is now at 1 Colmore Square.

In view of the fact that John had lived as a boy on part of the present site of The House of Fraser, it is interesting to note that Chesshire, Gibson & Co were

10. The Chesshires

asked in 1956 by Harrods of London to find a site for them in Birmingham suitable for the development of a new department store. They found such a site, bounded by Corporation Street, Bull Street, Temple Row and Cherry Street and negotiated its sale to Harrods. The store which was built there was first called Rackhams (the name of a smaller shop formerly on the Corporation Street frontage which had sold dress materials), but later changed its name to 'The House of Fraser'. I found this piece of information in an admittedly speculative short history of Chesshire, Gibson & Co issued by that firm in 1984, though I know that some of the firm's early history as stated in it is inaccurate.

As a young man John had to deal with the purchase of land for the projected railway line of the London and North-Western Railway Company. He also surveyed the proposed Sutton Coldfield Line and worked on the change-over of the Birmingham rail terminus from Curzon Street to New Street. He had had to go to London occasionally to give evidence to committees at the House of Commons.

He married Caroline Elizabeth Lamb at the Parish Church of Hartlebury, near Kidderminster, on 8 October 1839. She was born in Hartlebury and was about eight years older than her husband. It would be interesting to know how and where they had met. They settled at Eldon Cottage in Vicarage Road, Edgbaston, the first house on the left-hand side at the Hagley Road end.

Their only daughter, Adelaide Elizabeth, was born on 11 December 1840. After the birth and death of their first son, John Barnabas, in 1842, two more sons were born: John Stanley (known by his second name) on 6 May 1843 and James Lamb on 3 February 1845.

As agent in 1851 for Joseph Gillott, who became a personal friend, over the purchase of the Rotton Park estate from Charles Noel, John was able to buy for himself the best plot in the whole estate, the hunting park's old lodge, an L-shaped building standing near a hilltop in over an acre of land. It must have been he who had the old lodge demolished, as this is still shown on Map 2 (dated 1825). He replaced it by a considerably larger Victorian Gothic house which he called simply 'Rotton Park'. (There were then so few houses in the district that he evidently did not find it necessary to use the word 'Lodge' in the name of his new house, despite the fact that the old lodge had stood on its site.) After moving there he always described himself as 'John Chesshire of Rotton Park'. Adelaide, Stanley and James would still have been youngsters when the family moved there. I wonder whether they had a swing hanging from a horizontal branch of the huge beech tree on the side lawn, as we grandchildren of James Turner's did in the 1920s.

John, who was highly respected, became a Justice of the Peace. In politics he was a Conservative. He took a great interest in the Theatre Royal in New Street, of which he was a Trustee. He had a remarkably good memory. Even in old age he

The grave of Caroline and John Chesshire and the imposing Chesshire family tomb, both to the right of the path into Edgbaston Old Church.

could recite long passages of Greek which he had learnt by heart at school. He was always quick at mental arithmetic.

A keen member of the Church of England, he attended St John's Church, Ladywood. He became a member of the committee of local men who were responsible for getting St Augustine's Church built. After its consecration in 1868 he attended St Augustine's and was chosen to be its first People's Warden.

Caroline died on 6 July 1872 and was buried in a grave close to the Chesshire family vault, which was presumably already full, in the grounds of Edgbaston Old Church. Adelaide, who never married, must have become the lady of the house for her father after her mother's death. Her brothers would have left home by then.

There is a nice mention of John in a letter published in the *Birmingham Post* for 24 November 1934, the day on which the last regular passenger train ran on the Harborne Branch line. A Mr Wakefield, writing about Rotton Park Road station, wrote 'For many years, Mr Chesshire was the only* first-class passenger from the station and looked quite the country squire'. John would have been over sixty when the trains first ran in 1874, so he may have been driven to the station in his landau, starting off (in the wrong direction) down the long drive.

In about 1890, when his health had begun to fail, he had a ground floor washplace and WC built onto the Lodge, behind the conservatory and part of the drawing room, with a square storage room above it leading off the master bedroom and down a few steps. He retired from business but stayed on in 'Rotton Park', where he died at the age of 81 on 7 November 1894.

His funeral at Edgbaston Old Church was very well attended. He was buried in the same grave as his wife. Remarkably, there were *four* clergymen called Chesshire present at the funeral – his brother Humphrey, his own two sons and Stanley's son Reginald (born in 1869).

According to an advertisement in the *Birmingham Post*, his firm held an auction at 'Rotton Park' on 22 and 23 January 1895 of his property, which included a landau, some horses and five cows. I think that the part of his grounds which later became the allotments must then have been a meadow. The Lodge was empty for only a few months before it was sold to Frank Dudley Docker who was about to get married.

Stanley attended King Edward's School in New Street and then read Theology at Oriel College, Oxford. In 1864, no doubt recommended by his father, he had become joint Secretary with a land agent called George Mathews of the committee responsible for building St Augustine's Church, but he attended only the first of the committee meetings, as he must have been up at Oxford when subsequent meetings took place. However, I think that the neat copperplate handwriting in the committee's minute book (now in the Library of Birmingham) is his. He probably wrote the minutes up later from notes taken by Mr Mathews. Ordained in 1866, he became Curate of Hampton Lucy, Warwickshire, and was then Rector of Hindlip, near Worcester, for 32 years. He married Elizabeth Ann Pargeter and they had seven children, two of whom, Reginald and Cecil, also became clergymen. Reginald eventually became the father of James Hugh Cecil Chesshire, MC.

John's younger son, James, also went to King Edward's and then studied at Trinity College, Cambridge, where he was a 'Senior Optime', which means that he must have read Mathematics before changing to Theology. After his ordination in 1869 he became a curate in Kidderminster and then Vicar of All Saints' Church, Wribbenhall, near Bewdley, in 1878, where he remained until his sudden death in 1897 in a hotel in Ticino canton while on a visit to Switzerland. He was a bachelor and had left no will.

After her father's death and the sale of the Lodge, Adelaide had gone to live at All Saints' Vicarage with James. She stayed on there when Reginald succeeded his uncle as Vicar in 1897. A few years later she moved 'for reasons of health' to a home of her own, a house called Grassendale in Victoria Road, Great Malvern. Malvern's air must have suited her, as she lived to be nearly 96. Her obituary in the *Birmingham Post* for 17 November 1936 said that she had been a generous supporter of the Church and other charities. She and Stanley had presented All Saints' Church with a reredos (an ornamental screen behind the altar) in memory of James. She was buried in the same grave as James in All Saints' churchyard. I had difficulty in finding this, as it was neglected and almost hidden by long grass.

Neither of John's sons survived their father for very long. Stanley died, aged 59, in August 1902 in St Andrews, Fife. It is probable that he, too, died while on holiday.

Reginald became a Canon and moved in 1915 to become Rector of Areley Kings, near Stourport. Between 1915 and 1928 the Vicar of Wribbenhall was the Rev. Somerville Caldwell. Reginald's younger brother Cecil was then Vicar from 1928 until 1940. Between them, the three Chesshire vicars served All Saints' Church, Wribbenhall, for nearly 49 years, which must be some sort of record. Cecil had an even longer life than his aunt Adelaide. He died in 1971, aged 98. He, too, had made generous gifts to All Saints' Church.

John Chesshire had originally been intended for the Church, but family circumstances had prevented him from becoming a clergyman. No doubt he would have been pleased to know that both of his sons had done so and that one of them and two of his grandsons had given so many years' service to a single church.

* Not strictly true. Mr Wright also travelled first class whenever he went to London (see chapter 18).

Chapter 11

THE DOCKERS

Much of the information in this chapter comes from the book *'Dudley Docker: The Life and Times of a Trade Warrior'* by R.P.T. Davenport-Hines, published in 2004 by Cambridge University Press. I am grateful to the C.U.P. for permission to draw on this book for facts about the Docker family and to the Confederation of British Industry, the copyright owners of the photo of Dudley Docker, for permission to reprint it from the book. I have also studied the entries about Dudley Docker and his son Sir Bernard Docker, both of which were also written by Davenport-Hines, in the volumes of *'Who Was Who'* dated 1945 and 1979 respectively.

Dudley Docker.

Frank Dudley Docker, known as DD, was born in Smethwick on 26 August 1862. His father Ralph, a solicitor and coroner, held many public offices and was also an able sportsman. Ralph's first wife had died, aged only 23, after the birth of their third daughter. He later married her sister (despite the fact that such a marriage was illegal at the time!) and they had four more daughters and five sons.

DD, their youngest child, went to King Edward's School in New Street, Birmingham, but having come bottom of his form at the end of his first year, he left. He was probably taught by a crammer after that, but he never became much of a scholar. He began to work in his father's office but found legal work uncongenial, so by the time he was twenty he had set up a business called 'Docker Brothers' with his brother William, selling varnish from premises underneath the

Label for Docker Brothers' Gold Stoving Varnish.

railway arches near Deritend. At first they bought varnish, poured it into smaller containers and resold it, but later they acquired a factory on the corner of Rotton Park Street and Icknield Port Road in Ladywood and manufactured paints and varnishes themselves. Another brother, Ludford, joined them in 1886. The firm was eventually sold to Pinchin Johnson & Associates and later to Courtaulds. The factory itself was destroyed by a direct hit during World War II. Unfortunately several firemen were killed on the site when a wall fell on top of them.

DD and Ludford both became first-class county cricketers, playing for Derbyshire and Warwickshire. Ludford, who went on a cricketing tour to Australia in 1887, stayed on there for a time and was able to set up business connections in that country. One or both of them must have presented 'The Docker Cup' for cricket, to be played for by Birmingham schools. When he became too old for cricket, DD took up golf.

He married Lucy Constance Hebbert (b.1863), the daughter and heiress of a well-to-do solicitor, John Benbow Hebbert, at St Augustine's Church on 17 August 1895. They moved into 'Rotton Park', to whose name they were the ones to restore the word 'Lodge'. By then, 'Rotton Park' was the name of the whole developing estate and could hardly continue to belong to just one house and its

11. The Dockers

garden. The Lodge had become empty early in 1895 after John Chesshire's death in November 1894.

The Dockers had just one child, Bernard Dudley Frank, born on 9 August 1896. He was the only baby ever to be born at the Lodge. It is not known why they did not have any more children, at a time when many families were large. Bernard was always in considerable awe of his managerial father.

Lucy, who enjoyed going to the theatre and later to the cinema, managed the Lodge very efficiently with three resident servants, but stayed out of the limelight where her husband's business affairs were concerned. May Nichols from the next-door Farm mentioned meeting baby Bernard when he was out in his pram with his Nanny, but no Nanny was present at the Lodge on the night of the 1901 Census, though the domestic servants were named. Perhaps the Nanny had left by then, was non-resident or was just away that night.

The Dockers stayed at the Lodge only until 1902, when they moved to Kenilworth. In 1935 they moved again to Amersham in Buckinghamshire, so most of DD's highly successful career as a Director or Chairman of various companies developed after he had left Birmingham. He became an astute businessman who pushed himself very hard and made a lot of money. The companies of which he became a Director or Chairman include The Metropolitan Amalgamated Carriage and Wagon Company, Birmingham Small Arms Ltd (BSA) which acquired The British Daimler Company in 1910, W&T Avery Ltd and also the Midland Bank. He was an expert at arranging mergers between companies. He became a Justice of the Peace in 1909 and a Companion of the Order of the Bath (CB) in 1911.

He donated £10,000 to Ernest Shackleton in 1914 for his Antarctic expedition and Shackleton named a lifeboat after him. Shackleton's main ship eventually had to be abandoned, but all of the crew survived because they were able to get away in the lifeboat called 'Dudley Docker'.

But however well he did in business matters he failed to teach his son how to lead a similarly successful business life. In 1915, when Bernard, who had been at Harrow School for two years, but had left after having pneumonia, had been coached and was qualified and ready to go to Oxford University, DD decided to send him there 'later' (which he never did), as he feared that as an undergraduate Bernard might be called up into the Army. Instead, he sent him to work on munitions in one of his factories for the duration of World War I. Bernard was therefore able to play golf and have a social life outside business hours throughout the War.

Disapproving of Bernard's first marriage in 1933 to Jeanne Stuart, a showgirl, DD had her followed on a 'shopping' trip which she made alone to London while

Bernard remained on holiday in Scotland. As a result of what he found out about her movements in London he managed to get the couple divorced in 1934. He got Bernard appointed to the Boards of several firms and the Midland Bank.

DD died in Amersham on 8 July 1944 and Lucy died in Monte Carlo in February 1947.

Bernard, who became a KBE in 1939 for his good work as Chairman of the Westminster Hospital, did not marry again until 1949. When he did so, he could have made a wiser choice. His second wife, Norah (née Collins), who had already been married and widowed twice, was a former dance hostess, proud of her of working-class origins, who loved being married to a third rich man, being constantly in the limelight and being able to fling money about. Their many social activities, their commissioned yacht 'Shemara', visits to Monte Carlo to play the tables until Prince Rainier banished them in 1958 after Norah had torn up a Monegasque flag in a restaurant, their subsequent visit or visits to gamble at Estoril in Portugal and Norah's several over-the-top Daimler cars are well remembered by those of us who were around during the 1950s, when the Dockers and their social activities became something of a national joke. They moved to Jersey as tax émigrés in 1966 but found the islanders 'boring' and eventually returned to England, where Sir Bernard was voted off the Boards of several of his companies and the Midland Bank by shareholders. As a result they ran short of money, had to sell the 'Shemara' and return all the fancy cars to the Daimler Company. One of the cars had seats upholstered in zebra skin. When asked why, Norah had replied 'Well, mink is too hot to sit on'.

Sir Bernard had, however, been the efficient President and Chairman of the Birmingham Children's Hospital for some years before he married Norah, so my mother, who was a lay member of the Board in the 1940s, knew him slightly. I believe they spoke to one another at least once but never realised that they had both lived at Rotton Park Lodge.

Sir Bernard died on 22 May 1978 and Lady Docker died in a Paddington hotel on 11 December 1983. Her son Lance, by her first husband Clement Callingham, arranged for both of them to be buried in the churchyard of St James-the-Less in Stubbington, near Maidenhead, along with his own father.

The photo of Lady Docker, playing the tables in the Casino at Estoril in Portugal with Sir Bernard at her side and others looking on admiringly, was taken in March 1959 and is reproduced by permission of Camera Press (C/N) London. The caption which came with it mentions that she had taken a wardrobe worth three thousand pounds with her for their four-day stay there.

Right: Lady Docker playing the tables, 1959.

Chapter 12

HOW JAMES TURNER CAME TO BUY THE LODGE

The Dockers had left the Lodge in 1902 and it was up for sale for £4,000. The Birmingham Board of Guardians, of which my grandfather was a member, controlled the Workhouse in Western Road, off Dudley Road. Accommodation, elementary education and training for work were already available at the Marston Green Homes to the children of adults who were permanently in the Workhouse, but it was thought desirable to create another home for the children of the 'Ins-and-Outs', those who were frequently admitted for short periods. Rotton Park

A bird's eye drawing of the workhouse from the 'The Builder' Magazine, 31st January 1832.

12. How James Turner came to buy the Lodge

Lodge was suggested as a possible new home for them and my grandfather was one of a delegation from the Board who went to look at it. They reported that they found the house to be eminently suitable. The Board therefore planned early in 1903 to buy and adapt the Lodge and estimates for the cost of alterations and furnishing were prepared.

A long article in the *Birmingham Daily Mail* for 16 March 1903 gave details of the Guardians' scheme and stated that a meeting of Rotton Park burghers would be held that evening at the City Road Schools (opposite the end of Selwyn Road), at which members of the Board would explain their plans for the Lodge.

The following day's *Birmingham Daily Mail* contained a report of this meeting, which had been a stormy one. My grandfather was one of the Guardians who had spoken. The plan to turn the Lodge into a children's home had met with fierce opposition from the locals. A Mr S. White 'entered his strong protest against the unfair and unbusinesslike scheme of the Guardians to bring the children from the worst class into the midst of that locality'. A resolution was then adopted by a large majority, 'expressing disapprobation of the action of the Board of Guardians, and declaring that it would be an extravagant waste of the ratepayers' money to purchase the site considering the heavy burden of the rates and pledging the meeting to oppose the scheme'. As a result, the Guardians regretfully decided to proceed no further with the purchase of the Lodge.

I have discovered, by looking up 'Birmingham Board of Guardians' on Google, that in 1905 the Guardians bought another house, 19 Summerhill Terrace, just above Sandpits, for their children's home. There is a photo on the Web of children in the home. The house, which still stands, later became a home for elderly men.

James and Emily, their five daughters, two sons and a servant were living in 1903 at 3 Vernon Road, a medium-sized detached house which must have been a tight squeeze for a large family. Having liked the Lodge very much when he had visited it on behalf of the Guardians, James decided to buy it for himself. He had some alterations made and the Turners moved in during the summer of 1905.

The Turners in the garden of 3 Vernon Road, probably in the late 1880s. Winnie, Elsie, Dora, Emily, James, Daisy, Wilfrid, Mabel and Ralph.

3 Vernon Road. Barr Beacon can be could be seen on the horizon from the upstairs rear windows.

Chapter 13

THE TURNERS

James Richard	3 November 1850 – 31 March 1933
Emily Jane, née Poolton	8 April 1849 – 20 December 1931
Elsie May	8 September 1877 – 9 February 1937
Amy Winifred (Winnie)	17 December 1878 – 11 January 1950
Hilda Grace (Daisy)	29 July 1880 – 10 January 1963
Dora Mary Lilian	8 May 1883 – 13 August 1964
Wilfrid Gordon	4 March 1885 – 24 December 1966
Ralph Stanley	29 May 1886 – 10 March 1960
Mabel Violet (Mab)	10 September 1887 – 31 March 1920

James Richard Turner was born in Tiverton, Devon, the seventh of the eight children of Joseph and Ann Turner. Joseph held the responsible position of 'Manager of Water' for the Heathcoat lace factory in Tiverton. It was his job to adjust the sluices in the leat (a man-made side-channel of the River Exe, running through the factory's grounds) so as to keep the large water-wheel which powered the factory turning continuously during working hours. Ann made her mark with a cross when she registered James's birth, but I know that she did learn to read and write later.

Their children were William, Mary Ann and Emma, followed by two sons who both died as young children (one of them was drowned in the leat), then John, James and Charlotte. John was less than two years older than James and the two always got on well together. Mary Ann, John and James were the only ones to get married. I remember my great-uncle John and his wife Nellie who lived in Great Barr and I keep in touch with several of their descendants, particularly with their great-granddaughter Rachel Omotani, who shares my interest in family history. My great-aunt Lottie who remained in Tiverton used to visit my grandparents in Birmingham occasionally and also spent time with us if we spent our summer holidays in Devon.

Joseph Turner. *Ann Turner.*

William left for Birmingham as a young man and became a builder. Mary Ann moved to Birmingham to keep house for John and James. She married James Hodge. They had a son who died in infancy and two daughters, May and Annie. Both daughters married and each of them had one son who married and had children, so I have several distant cousins, with whom I keep in touch, who are descendants of Mary Ann's. I knew Annie Gunn well but remember meeting May Cheeseworth, who died in 1926, only once. I know nothing about Emma, except that she lived in Uxbridge at one time and later moved to Birmingham. Charlotte trained as a teacher and eventually became headmistress of Elmore School, Tiverton, and also one of the first two lady Deacons of Tiverton Congregational Church.

JAMES

James, like his siblings, went to the lace factory's own school, which must have been a very good one, full-time until he was eleven and then mornings only until

13. The Turners

he was thirteen, spending the afternoons in the factory as his father's errand boy. After that he had a full-time post manning the factory's gatehouse, where he was able to read widely and to teach himself shorthand. His handwriting and spelling were better than those of many modern children. In the diary which he kept in a bound notebook up to 1876, he wrote that as a boy he had spent much of his spare time making working models, including one of a water-wheel. He left Tiverton for Birmingham in April 1866 to join John, who had followed William in 1863 and was apprenticed to a Birmingham engraver. James had visited them for a week in 1864. Sadly, William had died suddenly in Birmingham in 1865 at the age of 27. James was evidently a good enough carpenter at 15 to find immediate work planing and fitting doors and window-frames for builders. One terrace where he worked for one pound three shillings and sixpence a week was Reservoir Retreat, off Reservoir Road in Ladywood.

Mary Ann kept house for her brothers in a house which William had built in Owen Street (no longer there) off Wheeleys Lane, but John and James moved out and went into lodgings soon after she got married, as neither of them got on well with their new brother-in-law.

Keen to improve themselves, John and James attended evening lectures on subjects such as chemistry, took examinations and won book and money prizes. They joined the Birmingham and Midland Institute and its Archaeological Society. John eventually became Director of Technical Instruction for Walsall.

When James was twenty he was unable, after returning to Birmingham from a Christmas visit to his parents, to find any work because of a considerable period of freezing weather, so he decided to set up on his own as a builder, with his office in a wooden hut which he erected on a yard in Owen Street. He grew a beard, which he wore for the rest of his life, to make himself look older and more responsible, sent for a former schoolfellow to come from Tiverton and work for him as a carpenter and employed bricklayers and plasterers as he needed them. He drew up his own plans for houses, adapting them from existing ones. He worked hard and moved the business to Waterworks Road, Edgbaston, next door to Perrott's Folly. He recorded his early building work in detail in his diary. He built well and many of his houses are still standing.

I have inherited a very large book, a typed and bound inventory of all the freeholds and ground rents which he owned at the time of his death in 1933. In view of the fact that he had lived at Rotton Park Lodge, which was built on the site of Rotton Park's old hunting-lodge-turned-farmhouse, I was interested to discover that by 1933 he had also owned the freehold of all the land on the right-hand side of Waterworks Road from the Monument Road corner up to and including Monument Retreat, except for Perrott's Folly and the plot surrounding it. In other words, he had owned the former site of John Perrott's house, later known as 'Monument House', and most of its garden. So he had had a **double** connection with John Perrott and Rotton Park, though he and his sons and daughters never knew or cared much about the history of the area.

I took a photo of the frontage of James's former office and yard at number 5 (after the road was renumbered in about 1904) Waterworks Road, and another of some of the 28 houses which he had built in Monument Retreat, shortly before these and the shops which he had built round the corner in Monument Road were all demolished in about 1970. I remember that the office, which was upstairs, had a somewhat Dickensian sloping desk with a high stool for the user, though it did also have a typewriter and a typist, Miss Annie Steed, by my time. I don't think there can have been a typewriter when my mother worked there between leaving school and getting married. She certainly never learnt to type and I have one or two copies of letters handwritten by my grandfather. The notepaper has the firm's address, but not its name, printed on it.

5 Waterworks Road, Edgbaston. Formerly the office of J. R. Turner, 1972.

The Karis Medical Centre now occupies the site on the corner of Monument Road and Waterworks Road where John Perrott's house and garden had been. I took a photo of this through a high window of Perrott's Folly in 2006.

Over the years James and his employees built houses mainly in Edgbaston, Balsall Heath and Smethwick. He retained ownership of many of them, managed them, did any necessary repairs and lived off the rents. He mentions in his diary that he acquired a horse and cart early in the Waterworks Road days.

His career as a public servant seems to have begun early in 1893. A leaflet which he issued while seeking re-election to the City Council, representing Harborne and Quinton, in November 1919, lists his services up to that date. It gives the following information about his committee work:

13. The Turners

    17 years a member of the Birmingham Board of Guardians; Chairman for 3 years
    12 years an Overseer of Birmingham; Chairman for 2 years
    17 years a member of Marston Green Homes Committee; Chairman for 2 years
    15 years a member of the Infirmary Committee; Chairman for 2 years
    3 years a member of the Workhouse Committee
    6 years a member of the Committee, Monyhull Colony for Epileptics
    Many years' service as a Magistrate in the Children's Court
    Elected to the City Council in 1912; served on four of its Committees
    Attended 457 out of a possible 463 meetings.

Despite this imposing record, he lost his seat on the City Council in 1919 to a Conservative. He was a Liberal and the Liberals were then out of favour. I think that his public service ceased at that point, though he retained the title of JP for the rest of his life.

On 7 July 1906, the eve of Joseph Chamberlain's seventieth birthday, James, as Chairman of the Board of Guardians, presented Mr Chamberlain with a congratulatory scroll on vellum in Victoria Park, Small Heath, now known as Small Heath Park. My print of a photo of this presentation bears on its reverse side a note in my mother's handwriting, to say that he did this purely in his capacity as Chairman of the Board of Guardians. As a Liberal he did not personally approve of Chamberlain, who had deserted the Liberals and become a Liberal Unionist. Joseph was driven round to several parks in one of a cavalcade of motor-cars on that day and received many other scrolls.

In about 1921 James offered £1,000 (a lot of money in those days) to the Town Council of Tiverton, towards the construction of an open-air swimming bath, as he wanted to do something for the young people of his native town. The Council gratefully accepted the money, which turned out to be about half of the eventual total cost. The bath, supplied with water by the leat, was constructed in 1924 in Leat Street near the Heathcoat factory, whose owner, Sir Ian Heathcoat-Amory, had kindly presented the necessary site. James, Emily and John attended the official opening on Thursday 17 July, 1924. The proceedings began with a public meeting in the Town Hall. There were some speeches, one of which was made by John. An illuminated address of thanks (now lost) was presented to James. After lunch, a procession, led by the Town Band, moved to the swimming bath, where Emily unlocked the gate with a silver key. Mr Huxtable, the Mayor, soon reappeared in a bathing costume, dived in at the deep end and swam a ceremonial first length, after which there were some further demonstrations of swimming. Unfortunately all of the outdoor part of the proceedings took place in pouring rain, so the swimmers were probably not the only people to get wet.

The Turners stayed on so as to attend a swimming gala on the Saturday, which fortunately was a fine day. I have a collection of cuttings from local newspapers about the opening of the bath. I visited the bath with my parents in 1928 and remember that there was a plaque on an inside wall recording my grandfather's benevolence. But the bath no longer exists. It has been filled in and the Red Cross now has its local headquarters on the site.

James travelled abroad quite extensively in and after 1888, sometimes with a few men friends and occasionally with some of his family (my mother and Daisy went in 1901 to France and Switzerland with James, Emily and Emily's sister Polly). I possess his passport, which is one large sheet of white paper, 11 inches by 15 inches, but folded up small. It was issued in 1888 and had cost him all of six old pence. It has no expiry date or photograph of the bearer. In the top left-hand corner there is a rubber-stamped visa permitting him to visit Turkey.

A fairly tall man (not quite six feet in his prime), James had lost some height by his old age. He had beautiful hands, of which he was proud, with strong and shapely filbert nails. My cousins Joan and Paul Beckett both inherited hands very similar to his. By my time James had a chronic cough and kept a spittoon by his armchair. He was seriously ill several times during my childhood and was at death's door at the time of his Golden Wedding. A subdued family celebration did take place, but we all had to tiptoe round the Lodge and whisper, so as not to disturb him. However, he recovered.

He gave each of his sons and daughters a house when they got married. Most of these were ones which he had built. He also gave my mother a terrace of houses in Grant Street, off Great Colmore Street, and made similar gifts to her siblings.

Though occasionally capable of laughter, he was usually of a somewhat mournful disposition, bewailing in his diary the fact that he was not a better Christian. My father told me that Grandpa liked to control the conversation at the meal table when all of the family was at home. If anyone dared to put in a remark out of turn, he would say '*I* was talking!' and shut them up. If he wished to terminate a conversation with one of his family he would say 'Bow-wow!' and walk away.

By my time he owned two somewhat ancient cars. As he could not drive, he employed a part-time chauffeur. Wilfrid was the first driver in the family and taught my father, Daisy and probably Ralph to drive. Dora owned and drove an Austin Seven, but my mother, though she later owned a car jointly with my sister, never wanted to learn to drive it herself. As far as I know, neither Elsie nor Mab could drive.

13. The Turners

James Turner's passport, 1888.

James became very ill in March 1933 and died at the Lodge on 31 March, a day or two after telling my uncle Wilfrid that they wouldn't catch *him* dying on April Fools' Day! According to *The Birmingham Mail* for 24 February 1934 he had left property worth £132,000. He was buried at Lodge Hill in the same grave as Emily.

EMILY

Emily was the second of the four children of Henry and Caroline Poolton (née Soden) who had two daughters, a son who lived for only three months and then another son. Caroline died, aged only 29, of puerperal fever soon after this fourth birth. Henry, who had been active for many years in the Old Meeting Sunday Schools in Bristol Street, first as a pupil and then as a teacher of arithmetic and other subjects, had to give up his work there after his wife's death. He was a 'Conveyancing Clerk' in the Town Clerk's office in the Council House, earning about £2 a week. He had a good knowledge of local history. The family lived at 8 Lee Mount, Edgbaston, a short road connecting the higher end of

Above: Emily Jane Turner.

Below: 8 Lee Mount, Edgbaston.

13. The Turners

Lee Crescent to Lee Bank Road. Although Lee Crescent and the houses on the upper side of it are still there, Lee Mount itself has now disappeared.

It is not known for sure where Emily went to school, but I know that between leaving school and entering a teacher training college in Cheltenham she did a year's unqualified teaching at St. James's Day School in Gough Road, Edgbaston, where she had probably been a pupil. She received a mahogany writing slope from the school in recognition of her service there. I inherited this and have recently passed it on to David Lockwood, the son of my cousin Joan. Emily's elder sister Polly never married and later on she lived with Emily, James and their family. I remember visiting their brother Harry, a ne'er-do-well widower who lived in Grove Lane, Handsworth, once with my mother when I was a child.

By the time Emily and James got to know one another at Francis Road Congregational Church (close to where Tricorn House now stands) she was already studying to become a teacher in Cheltenham but came home by train every weekend. They were soon walking out together. For most of their **four**-year engagement (during which James, according to his diary, had had frequent and serious doubts about her suitability to be his wife) she lived in lodgings in West Smethwick and taught at a school run by the glass-makers Chance Brothers, mainly for the children of their workpeople. She gained a Teacher's Certificate (Second Class) after an inspector from Cheltenham visited the school to observe her at work. I have all the letters which she wrote to James during this period. Some of them, in order to save paper, have two sets of writing at right angles to one another on the same side of a single sheet. By 1875 she had moved to the new Lower Windsor Street Board School in Birmingham, where she stayed until shortly before her wedding.

They were married at Francis Road Congregational Church on 18 October 1876 and rented a house, 11 Wyndham Road, now demolished. Elsie and my mother Winnie were born there. The

11 Wyndham Road.

family moved later to 28 Stirling Road and then to 3 Vernon Road (Polly died during their time there) before their final move to the Lodge in 1905.

I remember Granny as a kind and rather plump old lady who liked children. She always seemed pleased to see me and would regale me with an Allen & Hanbury's blackcurrant pastille, of which she kept a supply in a tin in her bedroom. She had a more upper-class accent than Devonshire-born Grandpa and pronounced 'cross' and 'off' as 'crawss' and 'awff'. She was good at crochet and embroidery and also at drawing, a talent which was inherited by Dora, Wilfrid and Ralph. I have a pencil drawing of a plaster cast which she did while she was at college.

Though a lifelong member of the Congregational Church, she owned both a rosary (she told me that she had occasionally been to the Oratory) and a copy of Christian Science founder Mary Baker Eddy's book 'Science and Health', so her religious interests were wide. Three of her daughters, Elsie, Dora and Mabel, became Christian Scientists. I have been told that this was a very fashionable thing to do in the early 1900s.

I like to think that Emily and James had a happy marriage, though he must quickly have made it clear to her which of them was the boss. My father remembered Emily tamely giving way to James over many matters. She was, however, a loving mother and grandmother. As there was a gap of nearly three years between the births of Daisy and Dora, I think she may have had a miscarriage during that period. For the rest of the early years of her marriage she must have been either pregnant or looking after the latest baby.

She once joined us on our summer holiday for a few days. I have a snapshot of her, which I call 'Granny in her natty beachwear'. She is sitting in a deck-chair on the beach at Fairbourne, busy with her embroidery and wearing (in August) an ankle-length black winter coat and a black felt hat pulled down almost to her eyebrows!

In December 1931 she was very ill and close to death upstairs in her bedroom. James could not get up the stairs, so they spent her last few days sending notes to each other. That was the sad ending to their long marriage.

Their daughters all went to King Edward's Bath Row School (actually not in Bath Row itself but in nearby Pigott Street) and then on to King Edward's High School. This school moved from Norwich Union Chambers in Congreve Street into its New Street building (where the Odeon Cinema now stands) while my mother was a pupil.

ELSIE

I have not discovered what Elsie did between leaving school and marrying John Plevy Harris, a manufacturer's clerk, on 7 August 1906. They had no children of

13. The Turners

their own but adopted a baby girl, Margaret Lavinia (known as a child as Meg and later, at her own wish, as Peggy), unofficially at first in 1914, the year of her birth, and then legally in 1927 after the 1926 Adoption Act had been passed. Elsie was a very quiet and self-contained person who was difficult to get to know well. Neither my cousin Michael Royce nor I felt that we really knew what made her tick. I once asked my mother whether Elsie had been unable to have children of her own. She replied that she didn't know. Some time before Meg's arrival on the scene, my mother had asked Elsie when she and John were going to start a family and had been told to mind her own business, so she had done so! John was a jolly man who could play the banjo. Peggy, educated at Edgbaston College in Bristol Road, was a 'bright young thing', a good-looking, vivacious and popular girl who was allowed to go her own sweet way. She could play light syncopated piano music very well. To my mother's disapproval, she turned up at her own twenty-first birthday party in a black dress and black nail varnish. The family lived at 38 Selwyn Road, a house which James had built for them.

Meg (or Peggy) Harris.

When Elsie, who had not seen a doctor for years, became unwell and took to her bed early in 1937, John insisted on calling one in. She died at home, aged 59, after a few weeks of illness. My sister suspected that Elsie had had cancer, but we were never given any details. John later remarried, had a daughter of his own and moved to North Wales.

Peggy, who had left home, married Norman McKenzie Milligan in Liverpool in 1937. My mother kept in touch with her by letter. During the War, Norman went into the Army and became an officer. Peggy, after having a stillborn baby, joined the Auxiliary Territorial Service (A.T.S.), the women's Army corps. Sadly, she died in late September 1941 at the age of 27 from injuries received in a car crash. I read of the death of 'Peggy Milligan of the A.T.S.' when the fatal collision was reported in the *Daily Express.* I sent the cutting on to my mother, who was able to find out that it was indeed our Peggy who had died. Norman remarried after the War.

WINNIE

My mother, who had won a scholarship from St George's Junior School, on the corner of Plough and Harrow Road and Beaufort Road, to King Edward's Bath Row School and had then gone on to King Edward's High School for Girls, stayed there with her long hair still hanging down behind her back until she was twenty. She spent the last two years as a 'pupil-teacher', which she said was rather a pleasant existence. But she had failed Matriculation **twice** because she was no good at Mechanics, which was for some obscure reason a compulsory subject, though she had done well in her other subjects. After leaving school she put her hair up and went to work for her father in his office. They became very close through spending so much time together. I think she was his favourite daughter. In her spare time she was involved in several good works. She left the office shortly before marrying my father at Francis Congregational Road Church on 25 July 1908. When they returned from their Lake District honeymoon they moved into their new house, 135 Rotton Park Road, where they were joined by a resident housemaid. There is much more about her later life in the next chapter.

Dora, Winnie and Elsie Turner.

DAISY

Daisy was christened Hilda Grace. James would not agree with Emily, who wanted her to be christened Daisy, so they compromised on Hilda, as the names had two consecutive letters in common. She was Daisy at home and Hilda at school. The main brain of the family, she gained honours degrees in English at the University College of Wales in Aberystwyth and Classics at the University of Glasgow, then spent a teacher-training year in Cambridge. After teaching Classics at Glasgow High School from 1908 to 1913 she moved to a school in Hereford. Her last post was in Wolverhampton, where she was for several years Senior Mistress, second-in-command to the Headmaster, of the co-educational Wolverhampton Municipal Grammar School. She left at the age of 48 to get married on 8 August 1928 to a widower, Henry (known as Harry) Cheeseworth, a retired Civil Servant, born in Devon, who had worked for the Post Office. He

13. The Turners

Hilda Grace 'Daisy' Turner, University of Wales c1901.

had previously been married to Daisy's first cousin May Hodge, who had died in 1926 of sleepy sickness during a post-World War I epidemic of that disease which had followed the serious influenza epidemic of the early 1920s. Sleepy sickness died out after that epidemic, but it could always reappear. Harry and May had had a son, Henry Douglas, so Daisy became step-grandmother to his three daughters. Harry and Daisy lived first in Oxford Road, Moseley, and then moved to a new house, one of a row of three which her father had built in Selwyn Road near the corner of Wheatsheaf Road. Oddly enough, the Cheeseworths lived at 28, next door to the Butterworths at 26, but sadly no Breadworths came forward to buy number 30! They later moved to Blake Street, near Lichfield, in order to be nearer to Harry's son, a University-trained bacteriologist, but he soon moved away to a new post in Surrey. Harry died at Blake Street.

Daisy was my favourite aunt, although she tended to age prematurely along with Harry, her senior by eleven years, rather than to keep him young. Good with children, an excellent story-teller, very well-read and an interesting conversationalist, she was nevertheless in some ways a family joke. For instance, while driving her car, she would refer to any other driver on the road as 'that fool'. She coached me in English when I tried successfully for a King Edward's Scholarship from within the School in 1933. She was a heavy smoker. She spent her last few years of widowhood living alone in a very cold house in Shirley (she told me that she could not be bothered to have central heating installed). My cousin Paul Beckett and his wife Marian, who lived nearby, were good to her.

Despite deteriorating eyesight, she continued to drive her car locally in daylight to do her shopping. On 10 January 1963, after putting the

Daisy married Harry Cheeseworth, 8 August 1928.

car away, she returned to the house, went upstairs, then collapsed and died from a heart attack, ripping a towel-rail off the bathroom wall as she fell. She was 82.

DORA

Dora, like many daughters of the Edgbaston gentry, studied at the Birmingham Municipal School of Art in Margaret Street and did very well there. Her only child, Michael, thought that she had stayed on as a teacher after completing her studies, but I have not been able to confirm this. I possess two different Christmas cards, with competent pen-and-ink drawings by Dora, which were printed for her parents to send out. She married David Royce, a motor engineer who worked for Herbert Austin, on 2 September 1911. David later set up on his own as an agent for car parts, with an office in The White House in New Street. He was an accomplished amateur photographer who did his own developing and printing. He also made some excellent black-and-white 16mm movies. Their only home, apart from a year which they spent in Richmond, Surrey, was a house called 'Thorne' with a big garden, in Cock Lane, Northfield. This house had been built for them by Dora's cousin Lance Turner (John's second son). Cock Lane was widened and renamed Frankley Beeches Road long ago and 'Thorne' has

David Royce seated (left) at Austin's buying office, Longbridge, c1910.

13. The Turners

now been demolished. I remember that it contained plenty of Arts-and-Crafts style furniture and some ornaments made of pottery or pewter. There was a water-colour portrait of Michael, who was born in 1915, painted when he was about twelve by a friend of Dora's, on the dining-room wall. Michael had an impressive permanent lay-out of Hornby model trains (clockwork at first and later electrified) in his attic playroom. When Dora and David had married, Northfield was a village just outside Birmingham with its houses lit by oil lamps. Electricity did not arrive there until Michael was about eight and no gas was ever installed in the house.

As Dora was married at Francis Road Church, I assume that her Christian Science Church was not licensed for marriages. David and Michael, who both had considerable health problems, got little or no sympathy from her when they did not feel well. Michael told me that when, as a child he fell, grazing his knee, and ran crying to his mother, she called out 'Michael isn't hurt! Michael isn't hurt!' a statement with which he was unable to agree. He got on excellently with his father but less well with his mother, who could be very awkward and had some odd ideas.

The Royces, who shared a genius for mispronouncing foreign names and words, used to tour Europe by car on their summer holidays in the late 1920s and early 1930s, shouting questions in English at the natives when they wanted directions to the next town. They also went winter sporting (Dora skated but did not ski) at St Moritz in Switzerland. At the time these were both unusual things to do. They often hired a houseboat on the Thames at Whitsuntide.

In 1937 David commissioned the building of a 36-foot motor yacht, 'Mirodor'. I was invited to go with them on her maiden voyage from Gareloch, near Glasgow, where she was built, to Oban and Tobermory and back. I enjoyed the trip but found it difficult to be compulsorily so close to Dora for days and nights on end. One day she would not speak to me. When I asked her what sin I had committed, she said that I had not dusted the cabins very well that morning! So I went off on my own on the day which we spent ashore at Oban. The M.V. Mirodor was eventually professionally sailed down the west coast and up the Severn and the Avon to Tewkesbury, as the Royces had joined the Severn Motor Yacht Club. She was requisitioned by the Royal Navy during World War II but unfortunately did not come back. I never heard where or how she had been sunk.

David died of bowel cancer in 1942 at the age of 58. He had had a lot of pain and various symptoms long before the day when he collapsed and had to go into hospital for emergency surgery. Everybody except Dora thought that if he had seen a doctor much earlier he might have had a longer life. Michael left 'Thorne' a few months after his father's death and lived alone in Edgbaston. He continued to see his mother from time to time but was never on the best of terms with her.

However, when Dora learnt of his plans to visit Leningrad (now St Petersburg again) with a British group, travelling in a French boat from Le Havre, in the summer of 1956 (very early after World War II for a trip to the Soviet Union), she decided to go with him. The party used the boat as a hotel in Leningrad, but Michael and some other men went on by train to Moscow for a few days and he sent my father a picture postcard of the Red Square. This came as a complete surprise, as they had not told any of the family about their plans. Some immoral philatelist had steamed the Russian stamp off the card while it was en route from Moscow to Birmingham.

Michael, who despite lifelong indifferent health and the eventual amputation of one foot because of diabetes, lived to be 93, was educated at Hallfield Preparatory School, Edgbaston (then at the top of Sir Harry's Road) and King Edward's School in New Street, his father's old school. He served an apprenticeship at the Austin works in Longbridge and eventually gained the professional qualification 'Member of the Institute of Mechanical Engineers' after several years of evening study at the Technical School in Suffolk Street while he was Works Engineer at the Coneygre Foundry in Tipton. He also worked for W&T Avery Ltd, the weighing machine firm. There were periods when he was not well enough to work and he spent time in hospital more than once. Soon after his mother's death he went to China with a British travel group. He left the group and visited several other Far Eastern countries on his own before coming home.

He married a nurse from Llandudno, Benise Lyall Emrys-Jones, on 21 September 1968, when he was 55 and she was 38. They had one son, Timothy John Crispin. They moved to Quatford, near Bridgnorth, where Michael ran a battery egg farm, 'Severn Valley Eggs', for many years. Sadly, Benise died on 27 March 1985. Michael died on 11 October 2008.

Dora stayed on alone at Thorne after Michael left. A local policeman and his dog used to drop in on her from time to time to check that she was all right. She was attended in her final illness both by a doctor who prescribed diuretic pills and a lady Christian Scientist practitioner who told her whether or not to take them.

Unlike her Christian Scientist sisters Mab and Elsie, Dora did manage to live into her eighties. The last time my father, Kay and I went to see her, she spoke to us but obviously had no idea who we were. She was described at her funeral as one of the characters of old Northfield.

WILFRID

Wilfrid went as a boarder to Tettenhall College, near Wolverhampton. He told me that as a new boy he had suffered at the hands of the other boys, because, having four big sisters, he had had no idea of how to throw a cricket ball but did know how to knit! He failed a medical for the Army during World War I, being considered to be delicate and unsuitable for active service. So he was sent to Glasgow and put in charge of a munitions factory for the duration. After returning home, he worked for his father in the office at 5 Waterworks Road and took the business over when James retired. He married Dorothy Walton of 23 Selwyn Road on 5 September 1925. Kay and a niece of Dorothy's were bridesmaids. The couple lived two doors below us at 131 Rotton Park Road with two black cats. They had no children. Wilfrid was a good amateur pianist and organist and he could draw well, mostly comic cartoons. Unlike his father, he had a tremendous sense of humour. He and Dorothy moved to Church Stretton in Shropshire after he retired. As James had done, he correctly predicted the date on which he was going to die. Very ill and no longer able to speak, he wrote a note for Dorothy in December 1966, saying 'On Christmas Eve I leave you' and did so. Dorothy went into an old people's home and lived to be 98.

RALPH

Ralph, who probably followed Wilfrid to Tettenhall College (I was never told where he had been educated) could best be described as 'whimsical'. Once, when he wanted some milk, he scandalised the Lodge's housekeeper by asking her for some cow-juice. Just because everyone else called my mother Winnie, he used to call her by her first name, Amy. He may have served in the Army in World War I, as his uncle John's three sons had done (I don't know how he could have avoided being called up) but if he had done so I never heard any mention of it. Give him a sheet of paper and a pencil and he would do a competent drawing of a liner at sea.

During my childhood he moved out and went to live in nearby lodgings but frequently came home to the Lodge. He was a partner in a two-man electrical fittings firm called 'Phillips & Turner' at 23 Cambridge Street. On 10 June 1933, not long after his father's death, he married Edith Flora (known as Nora) Brasier in her village of Claverley in Shropshire, after a ***nine***-year courtship. They also had no children. My mother told me that it was Nora who held the purse-strings after Ralph came into his share of the money and property which his father had left to his six surviving offspring. Ralph and Nora moved from their first home in Court Oak Road, Harborne, to a new house, which they named 'Tiverton' in Blythe Way, Solihull. In his retirement Ralph enjoyed gardening, playing the violin and the piano (but not to anything like Wilfrid's standard) and going on holidays. He and Nora once invited his niece and nephew, Joan and Paul Beckett, to go with them on a Baltic cruise. A heavy cigarette smoker, he died of lung cancer in 1960, aged 73. Nora lived to be 97.

MABEL

I never knew Mab, though my mother told me that she had held and admired me when I was a baby. She seems to have taught Domestic Science before marrying laundryman Charles Lockwood Beckett on 3 January 1913 after a **very** long engagement (a letter sent to my mother in 1907 congratulates both sisters on their engagements). Charles later opened a dry-cleaning business which he called 'Beckett of Birmingham', with shops all over Birmingham where garments could be handed in and a factory in Tyseley where the cleaning was done. They had two children, Joan Lockwood and Paul Lockwood. Mab nursed six-year-old Joan through an attack of influenza, then went out alone for a bicycle ride, despite knowing that she was by then running a high temperature herself. As a result she developed pneumonia and died, aged 32 – a tragic and to my mind quite unnecessary death. Emily had had to go over to Dorridge, where the Becketts lived, to look after Mab in her final illness. Christian Science seems to me to have done very little good to three of my mother's sisters.

Charles remarried and had two more daughters, Barbara Lockwood and Nora Lockwood. Joan, after a spell in the Women's Land Army in 1939 and 1940 until the death of the farmer for whom she had been working, joined her father's firm and was put in charge of the girls who did invisible mending. She married Stanley Gordon Jones on 7 June 1947 at Carrs Lane Church, Birmingham. They lived in Malvern and had one son, David Gordon, who has changed his surname by Deed Poll to Lockwood and is now a Ph.D. with wide interests. He was for some years a part-time tutor in Philosophy at the University of Cardiff and still lives in Malvern. As a widow, Joan, tired of being Joan Jones, officially hyphenated her second name and her surname. She lived to be 97 but suffered from Alzheimer's during her final years and had to go into a home.

Paul served in the Army in India during the Second World War. He married Marian Ellen Wilson at Carrs Lane Church, Birmingham on a bitterly cold winter's day, 22 January 1942, while he was still in the Army, but he was allowed to wear a lounge suit for the ceremony. However, he possessed no non-uniform overcoat and he and Marian nearly froze while travelling in an unheated train to a snow-bound London to spend their honeymoon. He spent some time working for his father and then joined the staff of a Jobcentre. Paul and Marian had one son, Antony Charles Lockwood. They moved to Westward Ho! in Devon after Paul retired. Antony has now retired from being a gardener on the staff of Exeter University and still lives in Devon.

The surname Turner has died out in our family as neither of my uncles had any children. However, my great-uncle John Turner married Nellie Hinkley and

13. The Turners

they had three sons and a daughter. His eldest and youngest sons, Percy and Leslie, were both killed in France during World War I, but the middle son, Lance, who also served in the Army but was never sent to France, married Gladys Baylis and had two sons, both of whom married and had sons. So the surname lives on in that branch of the family. Two of Lance's grandsons are brothers called James and Richard Turner, so my grandfather's Christian names live on, too.

Here is a list of the Turners' seven grandchildren:

Kathleen Elliott	5 April 1910 – 8 October 1970
Joan Lockwood Beckett (Mrs Jones)	8 October 1913 – 10 January 2011
Margaret Lavinia Harris (Mrs Milligan)	3 February 1914 – late Sept. 1941
Maxwell Elliott	8 August 1914 – 22 February 1927
Michael Royce	19 February 1915 – 31 October 2008
Paul Lockwood Beckett	30 July 1917 – 29 February 1980
Margery Elliott	born 26 July 1919

The photo of the Lodge on page 4 was taken by a friend of my grandfather's, William Topham of 9 Lee Bank Road. The landau outside the front door (you can just see the driver with his black top hat, in front of the creeper covered wall to the right of the window) was waiting for the Lord Mayor, who was attending a political meeting on the side lawn. A high string of flags and a few seated people are just visible to the right of the house, though they are almost obscured by parts of a tree. I have been unable to date this photo or to find out who was Lord Mayor or what the meeting was about. It was probably taken during the summer of 1906 or 1907.

In November 1906, during the heyday of the Suffragettes, Herbert Samuel, MP, then Postmaster-General, came to Birmingham to address a Liberal Party meeting in the Town Hall, which, according to the *Birmingham Daily Post*, was frequently interrupted by feminine cries of 'Votes for women!'. He had dinner with my grandparents and came back to stay the night at the Lodge after the meeting. Policemen had been stationed in the road outside the gateway before Mr Samuel and my grandfather left the Lodge by car for the meeting, to make sure that no Suffragettes got into the grounds. Dora once told me that despite this, a young woman had emerged from behind a bush and jumped onto the running-board of the car, shouting 'Votes for women!' as it went along the drive. From something which Michael said to me many years later, it seems highly probable that the young woman was Dora herself!

Chapter 14

STANTON MARSH AND DEVELOPMENTS, 1931-1934

I did not know the name of the speculative builder who bought the sites of both the Farm in 1931 and the Lodge in 1934, demolished both buildings and built houses on the Rotton Park Road and Wheatsheaf Road frontages, until Len Horton, who then lived at 147 Rotton Park Road, kindly gave me a photocopy of the 1934 conveyance of his house to its first owners (the price had been £700). The document told me that the builder was **Stanton George Thomas Marsh**,

Black and white advertisement for Stanton Marsh.

14. Stanton Marsh and Developments, 1931-1934

whose business premises were at 536 Hob Moor Road, South Yardley, Birmingham. I was pleased recently to find in a book published in 1998 by Alton and Jo Douglas and Dennis Moore a 1935 advertisement for Mr Marsh's firm, incorporating his photo. This is reproduced by kind permission of the authors.

I was able to trace Mr Marsh in *Kelly's Birmingham Directories*. His original business premises were in Pershore Road, Stirchley. He moved to South Yardley in 1931 and remained there until 1943 or 1944, after which he seems to have gone out of business, though he is listed as living at 38 Coppice Road, Moseley, until 1953. A Library assistant looked up some personal details about him and told me that he had been born in Gloucestershire in 1894 and had got married in 1924. I have not discovered when he died.

I found in Birmingham Central Library's Archives Department plans of the three houses (one detached house and two semis) all with garages, which he built on the Farm site in 1932 and those on the Lodge site in 1934, but I was not given permission to reproduce them. The architect for those on the Farm's site was Arnold K. Hewitt of West Bromwich. I could not discover who the architect for the semis built on the Lodge's land in 1934 was, because the corner of the plan where his name and address must have been had become black with age. It was probably not the same one, as the styles of lettering on the two plans are quite different. The only two detached houses, both with garages, which he built on the Lodge's garden were 137 Rotton Park Road and 24 Wheatsheaf Road, which is on the land's south-eastern corner. James Turner, you may remember, had sold a strip at this corner of his garden to the owner of the older house, 22 Wheatsheaf Road, who wanted to build a garage, in about 1920.

The other houses which Mr Marsh built are almost identical pairs of semi-detached houses without garages. However, he made a service road parallel to the two roads and half-way between them, approached by the then gateless back drive off Wheatsheaf Road, so that any owner could, if he wished, put up a garage at the foot of his garden, in about 1930.

There were not enough numbers available in Rotton Park Road for all of the semis, so two pairs of them were numbered 143/143A and 145/145A. However, there was one number too many available in Wheatsheaf Road, so the new and older houses separated by the back drive are numbered 40 and 44. The fact that the lowest house numbers in Wheatsheaf Road are 12 and 17 indicates that it may originally have been planned for the road to be continued later as a cul-de-sac on the other side of Selwyn Road as far as the Reservoir's boundary, but this was never done and the vacant site on Selwyn Road eventually had a house built on it.

I explored and photographed the service road in 1989 (it is now behind a locked barrier) but I could not find any signs on the ground of where the Lodge had stood, though I recognised some of the trees near the ends of the gardens as having been very close to it. Since then, however, my attention has been called to several interesting facts.

Ken Greaves of 145 Rotton Park Road told me that when his son Aaron was removing some crazy paving near the bottom of the garden he uncovered an open oblong concrete tank about six feet long, nearly three feet wide and more than a foot deep, with pipes running to and from it. Not knowing what its origin or purpose could have been, he called in the City Archaeologist, Dr Mike Hodder, who could offer no explanation. I was able to tell both of them that this tank had originally been just behind the Lodge's conservatory as part of a watering system for its plants. It had then, of course, been covered.

I had found in the Central Library's Archives a folded plan, dated 1890, of the wash place and WC and the room above them which Mr Chesshire was about to have built on behind the Lodge's conservatory and drawing room. This was very gingerly unfolded for me by a Library assistant. It clearly showed the tank, which was labelled 'Cistern'. However, the assistant said that without some very expensive stabilisation of the plan it would not be possible for me to photocopy it, so I just made some notes and a sketch of it.

I knew that the Lodge had had cellars underneath the drawing room, hall and dining room, as my mother had taken me down there once. Ken told me that the garage behind 147 Rotton Park Road was built over a cellar full of old fireplaces. A shed near the bottom of his own garden (already there when he moved in) was also built partly over a cellar, as his wife discovered when her foot went through a hole in the floor and she realised that there was nothing but air immediately below that part of it.

Brian Headley of 38 Wheatsheaf Road (next but one to the back drive) told me that when he was digging just beyond the end of his garden he came to some

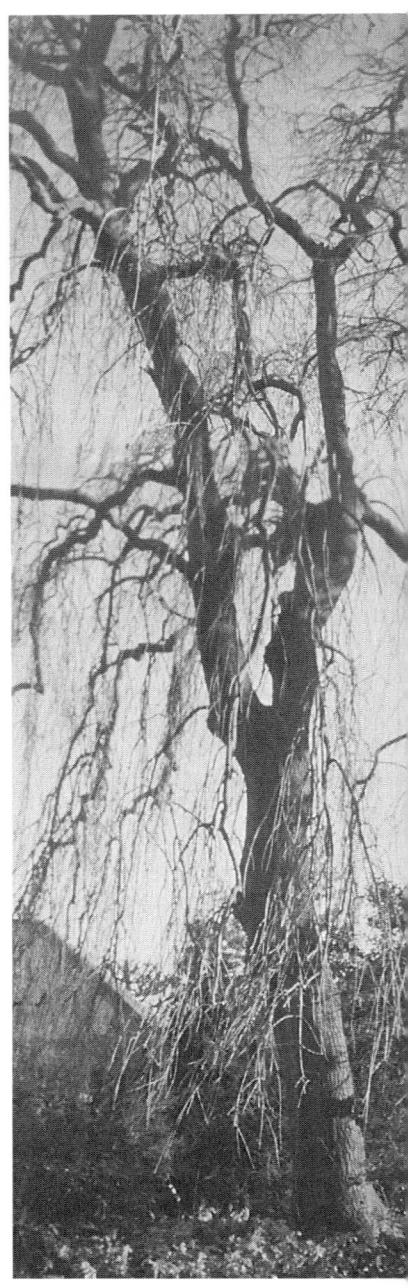

Weeping ash in the garden of 28 Wheatsheaf Road.

14. Stanton Marsh and Developments, 1931-1934

square quarry tiles about twelve inches down. I told him that these had been part of the Lodge's scullery floor.

All of the semis have long narrow gardens and several of these have mature trees in them. Miss Sheila Waite of 28 Wheatsheaf Road told me some years ago that when her parents were buying the house there were only two left

Left: Fritz Curzon, my photographer, particularly liked this road sign, which is probably as old as the road.

The three houses built in 1932 on the Farm's site, 2009.

for sale. Her mother, who was paying half of the deposit, chose to have the one with a weeping ash tree in the garden. Miss Waite kindly allowed me to photograph this tree, which used to be near the edge of the Lodge's side lawn, where I often played.

The tall brick boundary wall separating the Lodge's kitchen garden from the footpath of Rotton Park Road was retained, though it was considerably reduced in height, as the front garden walls of the semis, so was the Black Country slag wall in Wheatsheaf Road along the former eastern border of the allotments. Gaps were cut into both walls for the necessary gates. One of the front gardens in Wheatsheaf Road has now been completely removed in order to make a parking space.

When my photographer friend Fritz Curzon came to see me in 2009 about preparing the photos for this book, he drove me to Rotton Park and took photos of the houses which Mr Marsh had built in 1932 on the Farm's site and in 1934 on the Lodge's garden and also one of my old home, 135, built in 1908 by my grandfather and extended in 1934.

THE SALE OF 135 ROTTON PARK ROAD

My parents, who had bought 6 Meadow Road, Edgbaston, in 1933, sold 135 to a Mr and Mrs Hampton. It was they who had the garage, with a billiard room above it, built onto the house. Mr Hampton, a skilled wood-worker, panelled the walls of the billiard room himself. However, soon after he had completed this work his firm moved him to its Middlesbrough branch, so he had to put 135 back on the market.

The house has changed hands several times since then. I got to know the Holland family who lived there from 1982 until 1995. Mrs Madeleine Holland kindly allowed me to take some photos from the window of my former back attic bedroom.

Above: Taken from my former attic bedroom window, this would have been a view of the tennis lawn, the row of pines and the front of the Lodge in my days.

We moved to 6 Meadow Road in June 1934. An auction of furniture and effects from the Lodge and from our house was held at the Lodge just before it was pulled down.

JACK
Soon after my grandfather's death his gardener, Mr Tremlett, moved into the Lodge as caretaker with his wife and their two children, Winnie and Charlie. They looked after Grandpa's dog, Jack. In 1934, after the auction, they moved away, travelling in a furniture van to their new home near Bromsgrove and taking Jack with them.

Three days later, my uncle Wilfrid went to put his car away in the coach house and found a totally exhausted Jack waiting in vain outside the scullery door to be let in, having found his own way back. My uncle took him home to 131 Rotton Park Road and looked after him for the rest of his life.

Below: The view from my former bedroom window at 135 Rotton Park Road, with the Waterworks chimney circled.

Chapter 15

THE ELLIOTTS

My grandfather John Thomas Elliott (known as Jack) came to Birmingham from Portland, Dorset, in 1863, as soon as he had completed a seven-year apprenticeship as an engine-fitter there. His Master, John Towlerton Leather, a well-known Civil Engineer from Yorkshire, had been building Portland's breakwater since 1849, using convict labour from the local gaol. Jack signed his own name on the apprenticeship document, but Mr Leather was not present and someone else signed on his behalf.

Jack's fiancée, Jane Anthony, came from Wyke Regis in Weymouth to join him early in 1864. They were married at the Birmingham Register Office on 31 January and set up house in Ladywood. Jack worked first as overseer of the lathe hands for the Tangye Brothers from Cornwall at their factory in Clement Street.

They soon started a family, but being on their own in a strange town where there were then no clinics to give advice to young mothers, they lost the first ***seven*** of their twelve children (including twins) at birth, in babyhood or in early childhood. However, their eighth child, Edith; the tenth, Henry (Harry or Hal); the eleventh, Louisa (Lu), and the twelfth, my father Edwin (Eb), all lived to be at least 85. Bessie, the ninth child, died of TB when she was about ten. Jack died aged 71, also of TB, in 1913, so I never knew him, but I remember Granny Jane very well. She lived in my time with my uncle Harry and his wife Lottie and could remember the time of the Crimean War. She was slightly deaf and in a wheel-chair, but she was mentally very alert and lived to be 92. During Kay's period of study in London, Granny became ill and had neither spoken nor opened her eyes for a day or two. While Kay, who happened to be at home for the week-end, and some other family members were standing round her apparent deathbed, Granny opened her eyes, looked at Kay, said 'I thought you was in London!' and proceeded to get better.

In 1881 Jack was appointed Works Manager of the engineering firm of H.J.T. Piercy and Co, whose factory was on the corner of Broad Street and Oozells

15. The Elliotts

Street nearer to town. It had a plate-glass window onto Broad Street, through which a working steam engine inside the factory could be seen.

There was a building (now demolished) with the works manager's two-storey dwelling above the firm's ground-floor offices, in Oozells Street on the far side of the 1878 Board School (now the Ikon Gallery). The Elliotts moved in during the summer of 1881. In September the older children were preparing to go to the school. Edwin, aged three-and-a-quarter, cried because he wanted to go too, so in desperation his mother took him into the school and left him there. He never forgot his first day. The teachers, having sent the others off to their various classrooms, were obviously wondering what on earth to do with such a young child. They eventually gave him a sheet of cardboard with parallel slits cut into it and some strips of coloured card for him to weave in and out.

Years later, the building where the Elliotts had lived became part of 'Pantomime House', a theatrical costume hire firm. Kay was able, in the early 1960s, to arrange for the three of us to visit it. My father, delighted to see his old home once again, told us many details about the family's life there, such as the facts that his mother used to roast the Sunday joint on a wind-up oscillating spit in front of the kitchen fire and that as a boy he had had the Saturday duty of polishing all the knives on a knife board with bath-brick. He also told us that he had been brought up on left-handed bread and butter, as his mother and both of his sisters were left-handed.

He stayed at Oozells Street School until he was 12. Much of his early school work was done on a slate and with a slate pencil. He loved school and did well there, especially in arithmetic and music, which was taught on the Tonic Sol-fa system. The headmaster ran a small hand-picked children's choir which gave occasional concerts. Edwin sang in it.

He then followed Harry (who had already left) to **Bridge Street Seventh Standard School**. This school, founded in 1884 by George Dixon and housed in what had been Cadbury Brothers' factory until they moved to Bournville, gave boys a chance to study either engineering or chemistry and academic subjects related to them after completing their elementary education. Many engineering workers in Birmingham at that time, though highly skilled, could not read or write, so the school's regular output of literate budding engineers and chemists was an important new venture. The minimum stay at the school was four terms, but boys who showed particular promise were invited to stay on for another two years.

Edwin, like his brother, chose the engineering side. This included a course in Euclidean geometry which he found fascinating. He gained several large and imposing South Kensington certificates for subjects like Machine Drawing. But his father, unmoved by the headmaster's recommendation that he should stay on, insisted that he must leave in July 1892 after his fourteenth birthday on 31 May and begin to earn his own living. Children leave school when they are fourteen, said Jack. End of discussion. So out went Edwin after four terms, albeit with a glowing testimonial from the Headmaster. He told me that there had been no real financial necessity for him to begin to earn then, as his father and all three of his siblings were earning. Edith was a trainee nurse, Harry was operating a lathe at H.W. Ward Ltd in Ladywood and Lu was a dressmaker working for Lottie Jennings, who later became Harry's wife.

The school eventually moved into the Oozells Street School building, changed its name to that of its founder George Dixon and then moved again to its present premises in City Road, Edgbaston. It has gone through many changes since its Bridge Street days. Edwin and Harry, having discovered quite late in life that they were actually Old Dixonians, began to attend the Old Dixonians' Association's annual dinners, at which first the Bridge Street boys and then the Oozells Street boys would be invited to 'stand and take wine with the Headmaster'. They eventually became the last two Bridge Street boys, and after Harry's death my father became the only one, to stand. He was invited to make a five-minute speech about his schooldays at the School's 75th anniversary Prize-giving in 1959. The present boys groaned when he said how much he had enjoyed studying Euclid!

EDWIN GOES TO WORK

He began an apprenticeship as a lathe hand at H.W. Ward Ltd. After some months he took a week off because he had developed two black eyes, having been hit on the nose by a cricket ball bowled by Harry at a Church picnic on the Lickey Hills. When he returned he found another boy using his lathe, so he took the hint about what the bosses thought of his work and left. Although he could do beautiful copperplate handwriting, he was never as skilled with his hands as Harry, who could make, copy or mend almost anything.

Edwin then worked for six months for a jewellery manufacturer in Frederick Street, fixing small gold balls onto gold brooches. As he found it difficult to see what he was doing, he was sent by his boss to have his eyes tested and was prescribed glasses, to be worn all day, for serious astigmatism and long sight. The boss then said that although he would be willing to employ an older man who wore glasses, he could not employ a young lad with glasses and gave him the sack.

He was much luckier with his third post, which lasted for nine years. The German firm of Eckardt, Bendorf & Peine was run by partners Herr Eckardt and Herr Bendorf in Hamburg and Mr Morris Peine, a German who lived in Handsworth and

15. The Elliotts

had his office at the front of the ground floor of 16 Vyse Street in the Jewellery Quarter. This import-and-export company bought and sold small manufactured articles of many different kinds and traded with countries as far away as China. Mr Peine, who up till then had worked on his own, decided to employ an office boy. Edwin luckily heard about the vacancy, applied for the job and was appointed.

He and his boss worked from 8.30 a.m. until the day's work was finished at 6 p.m. or later. (I never asked him what he did about lunch.) He had to clean the windows outside and inside, light the fire, sweep the floor, sort out the post and deliver parcels locally on foot or by tram. The Hamburg partners frequently sent samples of various objects to Birmingham. It was part of his job to tour the district and find out which Birmingham firms made these or similar goods and what the prices were. He had to write all the letters by hand, as Mr Peine's handwriting was terrible. These were written using a special copying ink and then copied in a press onto a dampened page of a bound copy-book. To read the resulting reversed copy from the book it was, of course, necessary to hold the **back** of the page up to the light.

Ambitious to make progress in the business, he decided to learn German and joined a class at the Birmingham and Midland Institute, where he also attended a book-keeping class. He studied his textbooks in the evenings in the only warm living-room at home (the family then lived at 17 Mostyn Road, Ladywood) with his hands over his ears to shut out the general conversation. He made friends with two young men who were the Birmingham representatives of firms in Austria-Hungary and the three met weekly for supper and mutual language practice. He joined the Cosmopolitan Club in Fore Street, off Corporation Street, where on one evening a week nothing but German was spoken. He became a competent speaker, reader and writer of German, but his accent was never good and always gave him away as an Englishman. Much later he was made an honorary Fellow of the Institute of Linguists.

In about 1904 one of his Austrian friends, Max Zib, told him that he was about to return home to set up a business of his own. He asked Edwin whether he would be interested in taking over his job as Birmingham representative of the firm of C. Aug. Schmidt of Gablonz in Bohemia (now Jablonec in the Czech Republic), which sold artificial gemstones and other small objects made of glass. As the pay would be much better, Edwin jumped at the chance. Max Zib wrote to the firm recommending him and received a telegram in reply, saying 'Engage the young man'.

He set up an office at the front of 59 Albion Street (the building, a listed one, is still there) and had a stained glass window incorporating many of the firm's products made and fitted. He took on his first two employees, recent school leavers Charley Wildman and, a little later, Florence Nicholls, to be his traveller and his office girl. Both of them stayed with him until they retired, by which time Charley was Managing Director of the lens works and Florrie was the first Secretary of the private limited company, E. Elliott Ltd.

He made the first of his many trips abroad, visiting Gablonz and getting to know the Schmidt family, early in the twentieth century. The warm friendship between our families survived two wars.

In 1910 he left the employment of C. Aug. Schmidt and set up on his own as a merchant. However, he retained the agency for their products, for which he was then free to fix his own prices. On the strength of his good German he also became, in 1911, the first non-Austrian ever to be appointed as a foreign agent for the 'crystals' (artificial gemstones) made by the firm of Swarovski of Wattens in the Austrian Tyrol. He kept both of these agencies for many years, taking them up again after World War I.

He also began to import from Germany and to sell rods and sheets of a coloured casein-based plastic, Galalith. His first step as a manufacturer was to rent an extra room, buy a circular saw and employ a man to cut sheets of Galalith into strips, which is how a manufacturer of handles for tea-knives wanted the material to be supplied. Later, a similar material was manufactured in Stroud, Gloucestershire, as Erinoid and he employed girls to turn and polish small articles such as beads, bangles, electrical terminals, push-pins and handles for manicure implements.

EDWIN'S MAIN BUSINESS CAREER

If I were to write a full history of the firm of E. Elliott, which became a private limited company in 1936 and a public one in 1950, this would be a very long chapter indeed, so I will merely say that over many years he built up a flourishing business, doing mainly pioneering Bakelite and injection moulding and also spectacle and camera lens manufacture, with several factories in Birmingham (the main factory and the offices were for many years at 315 Summer Lane) and two in Walsall. For further details, look up **e.elliott.ltd.birmingham** on the Web. Many of his employees stayed with him for long enough to receive a gold watch for 25 or more years' service. He was always ready to look into any new process or opportunity. Harry, who worked for his younger brother for many years, once said to him 'If somebody offered you a new process for ***curing hams***, you would buy it'. My father laughed and replied 'I probably should, if I thought I could make any money out of it.' My mother once asked him when he was going to retire and enjoy life. 'The day before I peg out!' he replied.

During both World Wars the firm did much work for the Government and so in World War I he was 'badged' (i.e., he wore a badge to indicate that he was doing

15. The Elliotts

"RECORD OF OCCURRENCES" LOG

CB/R.4

Date: 10th April 1941

Address to:— Supt. Buckby, Kenyon Street.

Address from:— P.S. Wren, No.2 District Control.

Incident No.	Division	Position of Incident	Type Bomb	No. of Casualties	Time of Incident
B. DIV 00.40 / 1	B.2.A. 2	Friston St. nr. Ladywood Rd	INC	unknown	0036 00.45
00.30 / 2	P.S.24 2	Cambridge Cres: off Kings Eds. Rd.	H.E.	unknown	00.46 00.52
00.47 / 3	B.4.A 2	Belliss Street	INC	—	00.45 00.46
00.45 / 4	C.14.B 2	Portman Rd by Rotton Pk. Rd.	H.E	NIL	0047 00.54
00.36 / 5	P.S.Gosford 2	Alston St. Ladywood.	INC	NIL	0045 01.00
01.00 / 6	B.2.B. 2	Ranin St. Ladywood	INC	NIL	0100 01.02
01.01 / 7	C.13.B. 2	Loxlow St.	H.E	unknown	0050 0053
01.02 / 8	C.8.3. 2	"Elliotts," Summer Lane	INC	unknown	0058 00.15
01.05 / 9	14.B. 2	Memorial Hall, Summerfld Cross	INC	NIL	0050 00.57
01.06 / 10	C.15.A 2	Gillott Rd by Portland Rd	H E	NIL	0055 01.07
01.06 / 11	C.51.A 2	Rotton Oxchill Road	H E	Several	0105 01.19

TIME OF ORIGIN OF MESSAGE

Log showing the air raid on Elliotts in Summer Lane.

essential work) and was never called up. Some of what the firm did during World War II, such as making periscopes for 'swimming tanks' was so secret at the time that not even my mother was allowed to know anything about it.

Two different parts of the Summer Lane factory were bombed, in 1940 and 1941. Sadly, in the second raid all except one of the members of the night shift were killed. The direct hit destroyed the offices, so the company lost all of its records. The office staff of a dozen or so had to work in the billiard room in the attic of our home in Meadow Road, Edgbaston, for six months until the offices were rebuilt, which was particularly hard on my mother, who was also obliged by the authorities to take in lodgers for a time, as we had two spare bedrooms. The firm eventually moved to Bescot Crescent, Walsall.

Edwin did not manage to work until the day before he died, but he stubbornly remained at the helm until he was 88, which was his biggest mistake, as by that time he had lost his better eye through glaucoma, had become rather deaf and was generally losing grip. I was a (non-executive) member of the Board and remember how difficult Board meetings became. Often I would want to agree with my cousin Jack (Harry's elder son) when there was a difference of opinion, but felt that I must be loyal to my father. Jack, who had served an engineering apprenticeship at Archdales, was 59 when he eventually took over the Chairmanship, a post for which he had been in training for many years. He, more sensibly, retired on his 68th birthday in 1976. He lived to be 80.

After some difficult trading years the company eventually went into receivership in 1982. However, those (including many of my parents' friends and relatives) who had bought shares when the public company was floated in 1950 had by then done very well out of their investments.

CONSUL FOR AUSTRIA

From July 1925 until March 1938 Edwin was Honorary Consul for Austria in Birmingham. He was unpaid and had to send on any half-guineas he earned for signing his name to the Austrian Legation in London and also to pay the postage. Austrians needing his advice or his signature on a document used to call at his Summer Lane office. Our family met some very interesting people, such as Dr Bruno Walter in the Town Hall after a concert given by the Vienna Philharmonic Orchestra. Archduke Robert of Austria, a member of the Habsburg family, for some now-forgotten reason spent a day with my father at the factory and a night at our home in Meadow Road in 1942. (Thereafter, we always told our overnight guests that royalty had once slept in the guest-room bed!)

For several years during the 1930s my parents held Open House on the first Sunday evening of every month except August, mainly for young Austrians.

15. The Elliotts

These evenings were much appreciated by the many Austrian girls who were then working as maids in Birmingham households and had otherwise nowhere to go when they had a free Sunday evening. My mother used to provide a light supper.

Early in 1938, my father heard unofficially from a friend in the Austrian Legation in London that he was about to be awarded a medal by the Austrian Government. But immediately after Hitler's take-over of Austria on 12 March 1938, orders came by telegram from the German Legation in London for him to hand all consular business over to the German Consul, so that was the sad end of his consular service. However, he did eventually receive the 'Ritterkreuz erste Klasse' (Knight's Cross, First Class) in 1953, after the post-war Austrian government had found the old paperwork in Vienna and acted upon it. Two of his successors as Consul have received similar medals but they did not have to wait fifteen years for theirs.

SINGING

Singing was Edwin's main hobby in his younger days. All that he knew about music was what he had learnt either at school or in adult choirs. He joined the choir of Francis Road Congregational Church when he was 16 and was soon singing solos. Later he moved to Carrs Lane Congregational Church choir, back to Francis Road and then to the partly paid and partly amateur choir at the Unitarian Church of the Messiah over the canal in Broad Street (he was unpaid, but the New Zealand-born soprano Rosina Buckman, who was studying in Birmingham and later became well known as an opera singer, was a paid colleague). He joined Birmingham City Choral Society, which was conducted by Fred W. Beard, an uncle of the violinist Paul Beard, and sang in several of its choral and orchestral concerts in the Town Hall.

He also joined 'The Victorian Concert Party', out of which arose 'The Victorian Quartette' (that is how they spelt it). The members of this unaccompanied male voice quartet soon left the Concert Party and rehearsed and sang on their own in and around Birmingham with great success for sixteen years. They broke up only after Frank Dowling (who called himself 'Nesbitt' as a singer in order to please his employer) the bass, an electrical engineer, had in 1918 to go into the Royal Navy, which was so desperate for electrical engineers that they called him up although he was over 40. He went to Portsmouth, where he promptly caught typhoid fever and died. The other three tried without success to replace him and eventually decided to disband while people still remembered how good the quartet had been. All of them were married by then and their wives wanted them to spend more time at home. A bound book, now well over a hundred years old, in which they recorded details of all their concerts and activities, is one of my treasures. It has been read with great interest by my good friends, The King's Singers and by some officials of the CBSO.

MUSIC IN GENERAL

Edwin, a baritone who had also enjoyed singing with Birmingham City Choral Society in competitive festivals, was very much involved helping to run the Birmingham Competitive Music Festival from its earliest days during World War II (as was our whole family). He became its President and was also a member of the Board of the National Federation of Music Festivals which met periodically in London.

They had had a piano of sorts at home when he was a boy, but only his sister Edith had been allowed to have lessons. He told me that as she had no sense of rhythm at all she could never play anything properly. He could not read piano music, but he always derived much pleasure from playing by ear in his own limited way. While on his first visit to the U.S.A. in 1936 he heard a Hammond organ being played in a restaurant, fell in love with its sound and ordered one for himself. It was the first one to come to Birmingham. When news got round the musical grape-vine about it, several distinguished local organists phoned to ask if they might come to our house to see and try out this revolutionary new electronic instrument.

ST JOHN AMBULANCE

He qualified in First Aid during World War I and subsequently gave many years' service to both the uniformed St John Ambulance Brigade and the St John Ambulance Association, which arranged First Aid courses and examinations. He became County Secretary of both organisations and an Officer Brother of the Order of St John. He often went out in his black uniform with silver buttons on SJAB business on Sunday mornings when I was a child and I remember the smell of Silvo as he polished his buttons in the kitchen before leaving home. He resigned from the Brigade in 1940 but remained Secretary of the Association for several more years.

PHOTOGRAPHY

A good amateur photographer, he could develop and print his own photos. Later, he made many excellent 16mm movies, black and white at first and then in Kodachrome, most of them made while he was on his considerable travels in

Europe, North and South America and the Caribbean. He was always in demand to show his films to societies and organisations in the evenings.

In 1941, having never been in the Army, he joined the Home Guard as Birmingham's Garrison Film Officer. He had a conscripted Army Private working for him in the evenings. This young soldier would drive to our house and take orders before going to various parts of the area to show training films to Home Guard units, using my father's equipment. Although when he joined the Home Guard Edwin was too old to have a rank, he was considered to be an officer and was allowed to wear a collar and tie and brown boots with his battledress. Somebody from the Home Guard once phoned our house and asked to speak to Brigadier Elliott!

All of Edwin's own films are now in a national film archive. Bits of them have appeared anonymously on television, in the Birmingham documentary 'A Tram to the Bull Ring' and on *Blue Peter*.

ROTARY INTERNATIONAL

He was President of Birmingham Rotary Club from July 1941 to July 1942. During his Presidential year he bought and paid for a house in Selly Oak which became 'Sunnymead', a hostel for boys on probation, which was run for some years jointly by the Birmingham Rotarians and the Home Office. After it closed down the Home Office set up another hostel in Edgbaston Road for young men, not boys, on probation and named it Elliott House.

FOOTBALL

He held one share in Aston Villa Football Club, had two reserved seats with his name on them in the main stand and attended most of the first team's home matches for many years, even into old age, often taking Harry with him. As boys, they had sometimes gone with an uncle to watch matches played in a field in Muntz Street by a team which eventually became Birmingham City.

BIRMINGHAM SETTLEMENT

He was a Vice-President of the Birmingham Settlement which was next door to his Summer Lane factory and he sometimes lent his van so that equipment could be taken to one of the Settlement's camps for young people. He made a film of the Settlement's work which was widely shown.

RECORDING HIS YOUTHFUL DAYS

In his eighties Edwin spent considerable time when he was at home, tape-recording memories of his own early life and what life in Birmingham had been like round about 1900. Kay edited and typed out these reminiscences, which have been the source of much of the information in this chapter. Early in 1990 I lent them and some photos to the journalist Frederick Whitehead, who wrote and published six illustrated articles on Edwin's life which appeared in the *Birmingham Post* on Saturdays in February and March of that year.

LAST DAYS

After retiring he refused to move house and stayed on at 6 Meadow Road, along with our housekeeper Miss Nellie Cowley and me (my mother had died in 1950). He rarely went out, could not see well enough to read, said that he felt like a prisoner and did very little except watch television. He had always been a teetotaller, but after the doctor prescribed nightly brandy he used to drink this out of a medicine glass, pulling a wry face as he did so.

He was able to enjoy his well-attended ninetieth birthday party at home on 31 May 1968, but after a fall during the following week both his physical and mental health deteriorated rapidly. He was cared for by nurses upstairs at home until he agreed in October to go into a nursing home in Smethwick, where he died of pneumonia on 20 November 1968. He was cremated at Lodge Hill.

The memorial service for him at St Augustine's Church, Edgbaston (though he had never been a member of that, or of any other, church) was attended by many relatives, friends, employees and former employees, two representatives who came over from the firm of Swarovski in Austria, the Headmaster and another master from George Dixon Boys' Grammar School and representatives of several organisations to which he had belonged. The Vicar, the Revd. Philip Richards, well primed by my sister and by having read the many letters which we had received, gave an account of his life. A male-voice quartet of friends of mine sang (with organ) Schubert's setting of Psalm 23, a piece which I know that the Victorian Quartette used to sing.

I may have made my father sound like a paragon of all the virtues, which he was not. He had a few faults and could be very stubborn, but he was much loved and admired. He adored children and babies and they adored him. He was rarely in a room which contained a baby for more than five minutes without having the baby in his arms and probably cooing or smiling at him.

15. The Elliotts

HOW EDWIN AND WINNIE HAD MET

When my parents were asked where they had first met, they would smile and reply 'In the Workhouse'. Winnie Turner used to organise concerts in 1902 for the inmates of the men's and women's epileptic wards there (these patients were never allowed to leave their wards) at the time when Edwin was in the Victorian Concert Party, which once went to give some concerts at the Workhouse. They already knew one another by sight, because Winnie attended Francis Road Church where Edwin had been in the choir, but they never spoke to each other until that evening. It took them another six years to get married. My mother turned down his first proposal, saying that she liked him very much as a friend but did not want to marry him. (I believe she had hopes, which came to nothing, of another young man at the time.) Edwin proposed again in 1907 and they became engaged. Theirs was a long and very happy marriage.

THE WEDDING

At the time of their wedding at Francis Road Congregational Church on 25 July 1908, with the reception in the garden at Rotton Park Lodge, James Turner was Chairman of the Birmingham Board of Guardians, so Winnie's wedding had many more guests than those of her siblings. My sister gave a copy of the wedding group photo to Birmingham Central Library and I know of two other books published since then which already contain it. Everybody remarks on the ladies' wonderful hats. My mother received a canteen of cutlery and a mahogany music cabinet from the Board of Guardians. I still have the cabinet. The bride and bridegroom were the first couple ever to leave Francis Road Church in a 'horseless carriage' (otherwise known as a motor-car). They honeymooned in the Lake District and then moved, together with a resident housemaid, into 135 Rotton Park Road, a house which Grandpa had finished and got furnished just in time for their return. I don't know why they decided to call the house 'Altdorf', the name of William Tell's village in Switzerland. They removed the name-plate from the gate when war with Germany broke out in 1914 and never replaced it.

SWIMMING

During the first few summers of his married life Edwin, always an early bird, used to walk down to the Gillott Road gate of the Reservoir in the mornings and join some other men for a pre-breakfast swim in the deep part where the feeder from the Titford Pools in Oldbury comes in. He was not a particularly strong swimmer and eventually gave up going on his doctor's advice, after recovering from an illness.

CHILDREN

Kathleen, born on 5 April 1910, would have been christened Maximilian, after Edwin's friends Max Zib and Max Schmidt, if she had been a boy. The second child was due early in August 1914. But for this fact my father might well have been in Germany at the time. My brother Max was born on 8 August, four days after World War I broke out. My parents thought that in the circumstances Maxwell would be a better choice of name than Maximilian.

It was soon realised that Max was delicate. He had Down's Syndrome and had a hole in the heart, for which in those days there was no possible operation. My mother then had a miscarriage some time before I arrived, nearly five years after Max, on 26 July 1919. I was only seven when he died, but we had been good playmates and I remember him very well. Each of us was given only one Christian name, as my father said one had been enough for him.

WINNIE

Winnie (always 'Mother' to us and never 'Mummy' or 'Mum') took her duty of bringing us up very seriously. Both Kay and I felt that our behaviour and achievements had only rarely come up to her expectations. She did, however, have a sense of humour and we had some good laughs together, but we also got plenty of criticism, not much praise and were frequently told not to argue. However, she adored Max, who was everyone's darling and could do no wrong. We girls got on better with her as we grew up.

She was forty when I was born and in my time she was never in really good health, suffering as she did from a headache (due to water on the brain as a baby and permanent since her adolescence), lumbago, other aches and pains and a very poor circulation. The wonder is not that she achieved so much in her later life, but that she achieved anything at all.

Recently I received from John Turner's great-granddaughter Rachel Omotani a letter and a snapshot sent in 1901 by 22-year-old Winnie, on holiday in Switzerland, to John's son Percy, her first cousin. She, Daisy, and their father and aunt Polly had just got back from a mountain expedition. They had climbed up a glacier high above Grindelwald with several other English people, all of them roped to Swiss mountain guides. She describes how they had had to get their boots spiked beforehand and how the ladies had their skirts 'pinned up so as to be out of the way' while they climbed. They had had to jump over some crevasses a yard wide. She said what a wonderful experience it had been and that she would not have missed it for anything. She wished that Percy could have been there too.

A mountain expedition in Switzerland during 1901.

This was for me an introduction to an enthusiastic and obviously fairly athletic young woman whom I never knew. The only exercise which she took during my lifetime, apart from very occasional ice-skating and some ballroom dancing, was walking. Probably because of her headache she rarely read anything more demanding than women's magazines and light novels. She was a good cook and above all an excellent organiser. For instance, although she was no great needlewoman, she knew where to get dressmaking, sewing, knitting and mending done.

But she was a different person if any of us was ill, when she became a wonderfully kind and sympathetic nurse. I used to feel that it was almost worth being ill to experience this change in her behaviour towards me. She had done some VAD nursing at Dudley Road Hospital during World War I, but had had to give it up because of Max's frequent illnesses.

BIRMINGHAM CHILDREN'S HOSPITAL

She was the one and only Honorary Secretary of the Children's Hospital Brick League, whose young members, if their parents paid a guinea (£1.05) could actually lay a brick at a special ceremony when the next part of the Hospital was being built. She worked for many years with the Founder and President of the League, Mrs Florence Player, who lived at 28 York Road. Besides frequently visiting the Hospital and having to produce and send out a printed Annual Report booklet to all of the young members, my mother attended many garden parties, sales of work and other functions run by the Brick League's twelve branches in the Birmingham area. Before the Babies' Block was opened she organised the issue of free wool and knitting instructions to volunteer knitters from the League and our home was the clearing-house for the eventual one thousand white hand-knitted baby garments which came in. The Brick League raised £40,000 for the Hospital over the years.

It was wound up when the National Health Service began and was replaced by the League of Friends of the Birmingham Children's Hospital. My mother was then invited to join the Board of the Hospital as a lay member. Sir Bernard Docker, who was the Hospital's President (this was some years before he married Norah) took the chair at meetings. I believe that my mother spoke to him once or twice, but they never seem to have realised that they had both lived in Rotton Park Lodge, where he had been born. She was later appointed Chairman of the Nursing Committee, but eventually resigned from both the Board and the Committee on grounds of deafness and ill-health. Letters which we received from Hospital personnel after her death tell of the excellent advice and help which she had been able to give to the sisters and nurses and how much she would be missed. She and my father were regular playgoers at the old Repertory Theatre in Station Street and she used to buy tickets so that all of the Sisters from the Hospital could go to see the Christmas show there.

THE LANDLADY

She collected the rents herself from some of the houses which her father had given or left to her and knew many of her tenants personally. Sometimes she had to wait while a tenant took something to the pawnshop in order to get the money. As she never learnt to type or to drive, she employed a part-time secretary-chauffeuse during the 1930s to help her with desk work and to take her round to collect the rents. She inherited several houses in Monument Retreat after her father's death. At the tenants' request (they were prepared to pay an increased rent) she had ground-floor bathrooms, replacing the outside toilets, built onto them in 1938. However, these houses were demolished in about 1970. After her houses in Grant Street were damaged by war-time bombing she sent the tenants individually to see her own solicitor to help them to make claims and paid all of his fees herself.

THE RELUCTANT TRAVELLER

Her idea of a good holiday was a week or two at Weston-super-Mare, whose air suited her and eased her headache. She put up with the two long European trips

15. The Elliotts

Kathleen bricklaying.

Kathleen, Edwin and Margery (the author) sipping coffee.

by car which the family made in 1930 and 1935 because it was expected of her (though she did enjoy getting to know my father's foreign friends) and insisted that we took with us the wherewithal to make her a nice cup of tea in the afternoons. She declined invitations to go to North and South America with my father. After Max died she often went away on her own to the seaside for a week in February or March. When Kay, then a pupil at the Lycée in Grenoble and living in a boarding house, developed scarlet fever, my mother, who could speak only what she could remember of her schoolgirl French, travelled alone to France at once and stayed until Kay was well enough for them to come home together.

RED CROSS PARCELS

During World War II she and my aunt Edith worked as volunteers for half a day a week in the basement of Birmingham Town Hall, packing Red Cross food parcels for prisoners of war. The packers had to be trustworthy people who did exactly what they were told to do, as no deviation from the approved way of packing could be tolerated and they were handling some desirable items which they could not have bought for themselves at the time.

LAST DAYS

She was frequently ill during her final few years and died at home from cancer of the pancreas in January 1950. She had known for a month or so that she was dying. Once, when I spent a night looking after her, she could not sleep, so we talked all night and I learnt much more about her than I had ever known before. She said that she hoped that my father would marry again after her death, but he did not do so.

KATHLEEN

Kay attended Edgbaston High School (then in Hagley Road, opposite Francis Road) from the Preparatory School right through to the Upper Sixth. She then spent most of a school year at the Lycée de Jeunes Filles in Grenoble before studying French and subsidiary German at the University of Birmingham, where she gained a lower second-class Honours B.A. and became the first-ever graduate of the Elliott family. She served on the Committee of the Guild of Undergraduates throughout her three years and thus gained considerable knowledge of, and interest in, committee work. Finally she took an eight-month course at Mrs Hoster's Secretarial Training College in London.

15. The Elliotts

But there were apparently no jobs going in Birmingham for shorthand-typists with good French and German when Kay had qualified. After a few fruitless interviews she decided to fill in time by working for her father at Summer Lane as his private secretary and also as secretary to the Consulate. She actually stayed on there until after the end of World War II, during which the firm did essential work. She became a Director of the private company when it was formed but was never on the Board of the public company.

She was second-in-command to Mary Cadbury in the new Girls' Training Corps in Birmingham during World War II and also spent one night a week as a volunteer telephonist at District 2 Control, an underground Civil Defence post in Summerfield Park. However, there was never an air raid while she was on duty there.

After the War she left both the firm and our Meadow Road home, moved to 529 City Road and set up her own secretarial training college, teaching Stenotyping (machine shorthand) which she had learnt towards the end of the War, in preference to Pitman's Shorthand. She gave her girls an excellent training, but although the College managed to break even financially in some years, it never actually made any money, so after fifteen years she closed it down, sold the house, took early retirement and moved to 58 Oakham Road, Harborne.

She belonged to many local, national and international organisations such as the English-Speaking Union, the Birmingham Soroptimist Club, of which she became the youngest-ever President, the British Federation of University Women, the Girl Guides and the British-American Associates and was Committee member, Honorary Secretary, Treasurer or Chairman of this and that organisation's local branch.

For four years she was International Secretary of the Soroptimist International Association, working with Dr Violet Parkes of Sutton Coldfield, who was elected as International President. The duties of this important office consisted mainly of correspondence with Soroptimist officials all over the world, but also involved several foreign tours with Dr Parkes and the organisation of a big international conference in London, for which Kay wrote the bilingual English and French handbook. She knew some Italian and once wrote and read out a short speech in Italian at a Soroptimist dinner in Florence.

A Girl Guide since she was thirteen, she had to resign in September 1966 as Division Commissioner for Edgbaston in order to become County Secretary for Birmingham, but she had to give up that important post because of ill-health about a year before she died.

She was widely travelled. She made a lightning world tour by air in 1961, staying with Soroptimists and other friends in Turkey, Hong Kong, Australia, New Zealand, the U.S.A. and Canada. She enjoyed staying with her overseas friends in their homes, meeting their friends and seeing how they lived, preferring this to visiting art galleries and old buildings, though she did go to some of those.

She could play the piano, organ, piano accordion and ukulele-banjo and had had solo singing lessons, but although she had enjoyed singing in her school choir she never joined an adult choir. She did, however, compete several times as a singer at the Birmingham Music Festival (which she helped to run) and of which she became President, often doing quite well, though she never won her class. But, in 1963 the two of us competed in the Vocal Duet class at Leamington Festival and we won. This one success pleased her very much.

She had a succession of foreign girls living with her and helping in the house and with shopping. Some of them were sent to her by Bournville College, where it became known that any student who went to live at 58 Oakham Road would learn to speak excellent English, as she would get plenty of help and correction from Miss Elliott. Their nationalities were Austrian, Dutch, French, German, Japanese, Norwegian, Portuguese and Swiss.

It turned out to be lucky for her that she had retired early, as she then had several good years before illness overtook her. She began her researches into our family history, touring Dorset for information, and that of Rotton Park. She was skilled at embroidery, dressmaking and knitting. She became an experimental cook and enjoyed inviting her friends to evening meals.

She was Appeal Secretary when the Birmingham Girl Guides were collecting money in order to build a new headquarters and was one of the Guiders who looked after HRH The Princess Margaret when she came to open the new building, Trefoil House, in Brownsea Drive, near Holloway Head.

A long-standing blood donor, Kay was diagnosed as having multiple myeloma after giving blood in 1966. She became severely ill early in 1967 and spent six weeks of complete bed rest in the Queen Elizabeth Hospital while undergoing tests. After that she had to have regular blood tests and to go back into hospital for a week or so if one of these had an unsatisfactory result. However, she surprised even her consultant by the way she managed to keep going fairly normally between spells in hospital. She continued to drive her car until quite late on and she and I even managed to go abroad together three times. But by 1970 she had become increasingly disabled and spent more and more time in hospital.

On 7 October 1970, I visited her at the Q.E. She was feeling rather better and asked me to bring envelopes, stamps and a receipt book on my next visit, so that she could catch up with acknowledging subscriptions sent to the League of Friends of the Birmingham Children's Hospital. That was the last time I saw her, as she died suddenly the following afternoon from a brain haemorrhage. She was only 60.

She left money in her will for the formation of a Charitable Trust which would give grants to students, mostly for foreign travel to do with their studies. This Trust, recently wound up, helped hundreds of young people, many of whom were musicians or medical students.

MAXWELL

Max was sent away from home for a few days, probably to the Lodge, when my birth was imminent. On his return, my mother asked him what she had promised him. 'Ooh, a little baby sister!' he replied. 'Go and look in that cradle' said Mother. He did so and I am told that he greeted me with 'Oh, good morning!' (It was actually late afternoon.)

Always cheerful, talkative and very funny, Max was everyone's friend. My father told me that he could go up to the scruffiest-looking old man, give him a winning smile, say 'Hello!' and nearly always get away with it. An exception was a surly Father Christmas at the Co-Op in town, who responded to Max's enthusiastic cry of 'Hello, Father Christmas!' only with a growled 'Where's your ticket?'

He went to Miss Purdon's private school at 7 St Augustine's Road for some years but eventually could not keep up with the others, so my parents withdrew him and thereafter he was taught at home in the mornings by a governess. He never got very far with his education but he did learn to read and write. He enjoyed singing, acting in family plays, going to dancing classes at Norfolk House in Monument Road and going with me to the Sunday afternoon Young People's Services at St Augustine's Church. He was never allowed out of our house, though, if there was an east wind. When my father got home from the office and sat down in an armchair, Max would promptly climb onto his lap. Daddy would pretend to be annoyed and would say 'There are twenty-one chairs in this house', but really he loved it.

Once, at a family firework party (always held on 3 November, my grandfather's birthday), an aunt gave both Max and me lighted fireworks to hold. Max soon threw his down and refused to pick it up again. I hung on to mine. After a time it exploded in my hand with a bang, fortunately doing little damage, but leaving me in floods of tears and my father

Max Elliott.

furious with my aunt. Max had obviously sensed something sinister about the fireworks while I had not done so.

He had pneumonia several times. In those pre-antibiotics days it was a very serious disease, often fatal, but as he had always recovered before I was not unduly worried when he had another attack when he was 12 and I was 7. However, I was not allowed into my parents' bedroom to see him during this final illness.

I remember my father coming downstairs at breakfast time on 22 February 1927 to tell me that Max had just died. Although they had always known that he was unlikely to live for long, my parents were both devastated and my father never got over his death. Letters to my parents included some from complete strangers, saying how much they would miss seeing this friendly boy around.

Nowadays, Down's Syndrome children's hearts can be operated on and they can have longer lives, but I don't think Max would ever have made a successful adult. I didn't go to his funeral, which was on a Saturday, as the mother of a school friend had offered to have me for the day. He was buried at Lodge Hill cemetery.

MARGERY

I went to Edgbaston High School's Preparatory School in 1924 and on into the Big School for three years, then to King Edward VI High School in New Street, my mother's old school. She had moved from Norwich Union Chambers into that building when it was new and I moved out of it at the end of 1935, just before it was pulled down. I did well in the Lower School but took an unwise turning after School Certificate and was thereafter a disappointment to my teachers. Instead of concentrating on French and German, my best subjects in School Certificate, I chose to study Chemistry and Biology, with Physics and German as subsidiary subjects. In Higher School Certificate I got 'C' for Chemistry and Biology, 'C' for Physics and 'A' for German, which did not really count as a distinction, being only a subsidiary subject. I had not particularly enjoyed school and had absolutely no wish then to become a teacher. I had chosen the sciences because I enjoyed **doing** things more than I enjoyed sitting with my nose in a book and I wanted eventually to work in Chemistry. I left King Edward's at Easter 1938 and spent the summer in Czechoslovakia and Germany, staying with family friends.

In October 1938 I went up to Girton College, Cambridge. I graduated in 1941 with only Third Class Honours in Part 1 of the Natural Sciences Tripos, but I had also taken part in as much music as possible, having had a piano in my room, played first flute in Cambridge University Musical Society's Orchestra and sung in Girton College Chapel Choir and during my third year also in Cambridge University Madrigal Society, conducted first by Boris Ord and then by Dr Harold Darke.

15. The Elliotts

It was several years after I went down before I found and joined another choir as good as the Madrigal Society, in which *all* of the members had been excellent sight-singers. Most of the male members were Choral Scholars.

During my second and third years there was a War on and life was in many ways difficult and earnest, with much necessary cycling in the black-out and limited food. Few of the usual peace-time pleasures of University life were available.

After graduating I lived at home and worked for two years as a junior research chemist in the paint and lacquer laboratory at British Industrial Plastics Ltd in Oldbury. In my spare time I ran a girls' choir for the YWCA in Smethwick and became a Guide Captain. I then moved to Leeds, where I was an assistant to the City Analyst, replacing a young man who had been called up. I enjoyed the analytical work but could see that there was no future promotion for me in it without several years of further study and a difficult examination. I also knew that very few women were then appointed to City Analysts' posts.

I had had some excellent piano lessons in Leeds and by the end of 1945, when my job there was coming to an end, I knew that what I really wanted to do was to study music and then to teach and perform it. King Edward's had not taught music as an academic subject in my time, so there had never been any suggestion that I might study it full-time straight after leaving school. I had had my piano and flute lessons outside school. Women woodwind players were rare in the 1930s and I was my male flute teacher's only female pupil.

I was keen to go to London for further study. My father, bless him, was willing to pay for me to retrain, so I spent the whole of 1946 and 1947 studying very happily at the Royal College of Music. However, the Director, Sir George Dyson, allowed me only two years there instead of the usual minimum of three years, because of my Great Age (26) and my

KEHS pupil. Margery Elliott with her sister Kathleen, March 1935.

having already had one higher education. I gained ARCM diplomas for piano (teaching) and flute (performing) and also the Graduate qualification, GRSM (London), which qualified me to be a school music teacher. The GRSM course had included a compulsory two-term course of violin playing and learning how to teach the violin in class, as school music teachers are often required to run the school orchestra. I enjoyed this very much and made good progress, so I continued to study the violin and also the viola after leaving the RCM, eventually passing Associated Board Grade 8 on both instruments and teaching them successfully, though I never acquired a string teaching diploma. I could also play recorders and had had a few lessons with Carl Dolmetsch during the War.

I taught part-time in several schools in London and then full-time as a resident at Downe House in Berkshire, before returning to Birmingham in the summer of 1950. My mother had died in January and I wanted to come back home to keep my father company. I became the full-time Music Mistress at Dudley Girls' High School in September 1950. I joined the (paid) BBC Midland Chorus and sang in it for seven years and played flute in many Black Country choral and orchestral concerts in the evenings. However, I left Dudley High School at Easter 1954 in order to go to South and North America and the Caribbean with my father for three months.

After our return I never had another full-time post. I went back to Dudley as a part-time instrumental teacher and taught at home and in Birmingham, Coventry and Walsall. I deputised 26 times in the CBSO and played second flute to Delia Ruhm in Orchestra da Camera. I also played in the amateur Birmingham Philharmonic Orchestra on Sunday mornings and took part in its concerts. I went on musical holidays and courses in Austria, Germany and Switzerland as well as in England.

I studied for an external London University BA General degree in French, German and Music at what was then the City of Birmingham Polytechnic, which incorporated the then Birmingham School of Music (now Birmingham City University) and graduated with an Upper Second Class degree in 1973. I still did some teaching and took part in various choirs and orchestras during these three years. I was a member of the Birmingham Bach Choir for a time and of the City of Birmingham Choir for 35 years and of several smaller occasional choral groups such as the Easter Singers and the Priory Singers of Coventry. Though my voice was not at first very powerful, after some excellent solo singing lessons with Helen Henschel, I gained diplomas as a solo singer and teacher and took part in three recitals organised by the Recital Club in Birmingham, the last two of them with my former school friend Beryl Chempin (née Perry) as accompanist. I went weekly to London on Mondays for several years to sing in the London Bach

15. The Elliotts

Society's Choir under Dr Paul Steinitz and went abroad with that choir three times. I have sung in various choirs in Australia, Austria, Bulgaria, Canada, Germany, Italy and Spain.

Like my sister, who had taught me to touch-type when I was twenty, I also became Hon. Secretary of various organisations and Editor of several newsletters including The King's Singers' UK newsletter, and of two club magazines.

After my father died I sold our Meadow Road home and moved into a small modern Bryant house in Christchurch Close, Edgbaston. I had been there for less than two years when Kay died. I decided to move again into her somewhat larger house in Oakham Road, Harborne, where I inherited her two cats. Several students stayed with me while I was there. I sold the house in 2007 and moved into the sheltered accommodation for old people where I now live happily in my own bungalow.

I was made an Honorary Fellow of Birmingham Conservatoire in 2004 for my 'lifetime involvement in music-making in Birmingham and the West Midlands'. Unfortunately I have gone very deaf with age, as both of my parents did, so music is no longer my major interest and nowadays I go to few concerts and have got rid of all my instruments except an upright piano.

My only claim to fame is that I have taken part in various TV and radio quizzes. I was a semi-finalist in the second series of BBC TV's 'Mastermind' in 1973, missing a place in the Final by one point after a tie and the programme's first sudden-death play-off. I took part in two series of 'Brain of Britain' on Radio 4, reaching the Final and coming third out of four both times.

My father put me on the Board of the public limited company, E. Elliott Ltd, when it was floated. I had worked in his office during most of the Long Vacation in 1940. I went abroad on the firm's behalf twice, to Montpellier in southern France with the Sales Director and to Amsterdam on my own as English-German interpreter on the British Plastics Federation's stand at a plastics exhibition.

I am the last of the Elliotts. My aunt Edith never married. My aunt Louisa married Walter Henry Collins and had twin sons, Walter and Edwin. Walter married and had a daughter and two sons, all of whom married, but I have lost touch with them, though I know that the younger son settled in Australia. Anyway, their name is not Elliott. My uncle Harry and his wife Lottie had two sons – Jack, who married Kathleen Lilian Dingley but had no children, and Bob, who was epileptic and never married, so the Elliott family founded by Jack Elliott and Jane Anthony from Portland will die out when I do.

Chapter 16

THE TENNIS CLUB, THE SQUASH CLUB AND DEVELOPMENTS, 2013-2014

There was a tennis lawn immediately behind the garden of our house in 1908, when it was the only house between the Lodge and the corner of Selwyn Road. It belonged to my grandfather who didn't know who had laid the tennis lawn out. The Lodge's garden already had two lawns big enough for tennis, although the Lodge was built well before the development, largely in Ampton Road, Edgbaston, of the game of Lawn Tennis. Terry Slater, in his book *'Edgbaston – A History'*, says that many local gardens acquired tennis lawns quite soon after the game came into being in the 1870s.

When the row of semis, 133 to 119, was completed by 1911, a space was left between 123 and 119 for an entrance drive to what must by then have been two tennis courts. Someone must have been thinking about creating a tennis club, but I have not been able to find out who it was. (The semis originally had no garages but all of them appear to have acquired one since then by alteration to the side entry and the coal storage area.) The corner site with Selwyn Road was still a field with hedges onto the two roads when we left Rotton Park Road in 1934. Justin Pinkess of 17 Wheatsheaf Road tells me that his sister Stella used to pick blackberries in that field after crawling in through a hole in the hedge. Number 2 Selwyn Road was built diagonally across the corner some time after 1934.

The Portland Lawn Tennis Club was first mentioned in *Kelly's Birmingham Directory* in 1913. Its secretary was Dr Edmund Whichello of 174 Rotton Park Road.

By the time I remember the Club in the 1920s it had two red hard courts, each surrounded by a high wire-netting fence, end to end at different levels on the hill and both reached by a path immediately behind the Rotton Park Road gardens. The gardens of the older houses in Wheatsheaf Road backed onto the other side of

Top: The Squash Club's building.

Bottom: The path to the Squash Club between 123 and 121 Rotton Park Road, before 2004.

'Wilderness'.

the courts. There was a small pavilion on the Selwyn Road side. My sister became a member in the late 1920s.

By 1959 the Club had changed its name to the Wingate Tennis Club and I have been told that its membership thereafter was mainly Jewish.

The site was then sold and levelled for the construction of The Birmingham Squash and Social Club, which opened in 1971 and changed its name slightly several times. Its Manager, the late Dave Hickman, told me that there had been some difficulty in getting a licence for the bar because of Joseph Gillott's ban on the sale of alcohol on his estate.

The Squash Club bought from Mr Cartwright, the owner of 24 Wheatsheaf Road, a plot of unused land between the bottom of his garden and the bottoms of the gardens of 135 and 137 Rotton Park Road, in order to make a car park. There were local objections and no such car park was ever constructed. So this plot, which stood higher than the levelled site of the Squash Club itself, was separated off from it by a brick wall over four feet high and left to run wild. I was surprised to find a 'wilderness' with brambles, weeds and a pine tree so close to suburban Rotton Park Road.

16. The Tennis Club, the Squash Club and Developments, 2013-2014

The Squash Club closed down in August 2004. In 2005 a building firm, Timpglow Ltd of Henley-in-Arden, sought permission to construct 17 dwellings of various sizes on its site and to demolish 119 Rotton Park Road in order to make a wider access road to these. My records tell me that despite more local objections this scheme was approved with conditions in July 2005, but no such work was done, probably because of the general slump in house-building. The Squash Club's building remained derelict, with a large rubbish heap beside it, behind a tall locked gate, until 2013. However, on the opposite side of the road there was still a signpost pointing to the 'Squash and Health Club'.

UPDATE, 2013-2014

As I no longer drive, I had not been to Rotton Park Road for some time. I was interested to read in the Property supplement to the *Birmingham Post* on 18 April 2013 an advertisement for '**Edgbaston Gate**', a new gated development of twelve houses now being built 'just off Rotton Park Road' by a firm called St Nicholas Developments Ltd. I phoned the office of the joint selling agent, Robert Powell, and was told that this development is, as I had thought it must be, on the site of the Squash Club. I was sent an illustrated prospectus and have now been round there several times to have a look. I had not even known that the Squash Club had been demolished. This had happened only just before building began.

Edgbaston Gate.

On my first visit I was shown round an impressive semi-detached show house by a lady from Robert Powell's, but I was able to explore only part of the rest of the site, as most of it was a 'hard hat only' area behind wire netting. The semis on the site of the Squash Club's building were then still covered with scaffolding. The plan comes from the prospectus and the picture of the show house from the *Birmingham Post* advertisement. The later photos were taken by my goddaughter, Sarah Bond.

The access drive between 123 and 119 Rotton Park Road has been slightly widened, apparently by the partial reduction of 119. The nearby front gardens in Rotton Park Road have been bevelled off with re-positioned walls, so that cars leaving through the electrically-controlled gate will have room to wait safely outside it before emerging into the road, which is often busy. There are hard parking spaces, but no garages, on the new development.

The detached house at the northern end has a bigger garden than any of the others, as it will be next to 'The Wilderness', the site of the Squash Club's intended, but never constructed, car park. Trees will be preserved wherever possible. By mid-January 2014 all of the houses had been sold or reserved.

I observed with some amusement that the signpost pointing to the 'Squash and Health Club' was **still** there, nine years after that Club had closed down. The lady from Robert Powell's had not noticed it until I pointed it out to her. I have now heard that by February 2014 it had at last disappeared and been replaced by one saying 'Edgbaston Gate'.

Access drive from Rotton Park Road into Edgbaston Gate.

Chapter 17

ROTTON PARK ROAD STATION

The Harborne Branch railway ran a passenger service to Birmingham New Street station between 1874 and 1934. As Rotton Park Road station on this branch was dismantled soon after the service ceased, present-day residents of Rotton Park probably have no idea of what it looked like, so I am including a chapter about it, with two photos which the Birmingham-based railway photographer and enthusiast W.A. Camwell took on 22 November 1934, the very last day of the service. These are reproduced by kind permission of The Stephenson Locomotive Society. Photo 3519 shows the last-ever regular train from New Street to Harborne standing at the station.

When I was a young child no buses ran along Portland Road. To get to town by public transport we had either to walk to Hagley Road and catch a number 34 tram which went via Islington Row, Bath Row and Holloway Head towards Navigation Street (later, a number 6 or 9 bus which went down Broad Street to New Street and Corporation Street) or to go by train to New Street station. Before he had a car my father used to travel by train to Monument Lane station and walk from there to his office in the Jewellery Quarter.

Whole station (left) and train at platform (right). Photos by W.A. Camwell courtesy of SLS Library Station Collection.

A train from Harborne approaching Hagley Road station. Photo courtesy D.J.M. Smith and D. Harrison, The Harborne Express, Brewin Books.

The Harborne Branch was a single line leaving the main Stour Valley (New Street to Wolverhampton) Line by a bridge over the Birmingham Canal just beyond Monument Lane, with stations at Icknield Port Road, Rotton Park Road and Hagley Road and its terminus in Station Road, Harborne. We lived close enough to the railway to be able to hear occasional chuff-chuff noises and engine whistles. No trains ran on Sundays. On 1 January 1923, when the many different railway companies in the country were condensed into just four, it became part of the London, Midland and Scottish (LMS) Railway system.

Rotton Park Road station, which originally had only one platform, was rebuilt in 1903 with up and down platforms inside the only loop line on the whole of the Harborne Branch. As a train came in, the porter would stand near the edge of the platform, holding up in his right hand a cylindrical metal staff about two feet long with some thicker rings on it. This would be accepted by the engine driver, who would put a different staff into the porter's left hand. The porter would then insert the new staff into the mechanism for changing the points and alter them.

The entrance to the station was on the east side of Rotton Park Road, a few yards north of the corner of Gillott Road. A fairly long walkway ran on high trestles at right angles to the road. This led to a footbridge on the left over the southern track and a staircase on the right down to the building and platforms. It was also possible to approach the station from the bridge in Selwyn Road, by going down a

17. Rotton Park Road Station

staircase onto a path alongside the railway (but separated from it by a fence) and then up another staircase to the same footbridge over the southern track.

The station had a ticket office, two waiting rooms (one general and one for ladies only), the station-master's office, a penny-in-the-slot chocolate machine, two name boards, the point-changing mechanism and not much else. Although *Kelly's Birmingham Directories* always included the name of the current station-master, he obviously could not and did not live there.

When I went to King Edward VI High School in New Street in 1931 I used to go there by train. About ten or twelve KE girls, most of whom got in at Harborne, usually travelled together. The trains had separate compartments, each holding twelve passengers, but on one memorable occasion we travelled in a corridor coach which had apparently got there by mistake.

Passenger trains ceased to run on 22 November 1934, after a couple of months' notice had been given. One reason was that city-bound trains, which ran rather slowly anyhow (hence the line's affectionate nickname, 'The Harborne Express') often had to wait at Icknield Port Road station for a late-running main-line train to go past first. More buses were running by that time and they were found to be a quicker way of getting into town. However, the line continued to be used for goods and coal until Dr Beeching's axe fell on it in 1963.

Mitchells & Butlers' brewery in Cape Hill had its own spur which left the Harborne Branch at a triangular junction just west of Rotton Park Road. The brewery also had its own engine, 'John Barleycorn'. Charles Darby, a former Managing Director of M&B, tells me that until the spur was closed down in 1962 regular supplies of malt, which came from Bedford, used to arrive by rail.

The old line, minus its rails, after some years of being used as an unofficial rubbish dump, was cleaned up and replaced between Harborne and Selwyn Road by the Harborne Walkway, which was opened in 1981 and now shows no signs of having ever been a railway. The cutting between the far ends of the Gillott Road gardens and Summerfield Park was added to the Park in 1976 and was filled in and grassed over for reasons of safety.

Hallewell Road, from Rotton Park Road to Selwyn Road, was cut parallel to the railway late in 1906 and was named after Sir Hallewell Rogers (1864-1931), who had been Lord Mayor from 1904 to 1905 and also MP for Moseley.

Some of the information in this chapter comes from the book *'The Harborne Express'* by Donald Smith and Derek Harrison, published by Brewin Books Ltd. in 1995.

Chapter 18

SOME DISTINGUISHED INHABITANTS OF ROTTON PARK

It was suggested to me that a chapter on Rotton Park residents who became well known or showed some unusual characteristic or accomplishment would be of general interest. I have found it impossible to produce a comprehensive list but have done my best, although I have not been able to find out all of the relevant dates. I also realise that I must have left out many people who are worthy of mention.

OUR NEXT-DOOR NEIGHBOURS AT 133 ROTTON PARK ROAD

Oscar Deutsch (1893-1941), founder and owner of the Odeon Cinema chain, and his wife **Lily**, who chose the decor and colour schemes for the interior of his cinemas, lived at 133 during my early childhood and later moved to 8 Rotton Park Road. Their eldest son Ronnie was a playmate of mine. Ronnie and I met again in 1995 when he came to unveil a blue plaque dedicated to his father outside the former first Odeon Cinema in Birchfield Road, Perry Barr.

Leon David Abrams (1924-2012) was the eldest child of Sam and Emmie Abrams, who moved in after the Deutsch family left. He was also a playmate of mine and we renewed contact by letter while I was writing this book. Sadly, this was not long before he died. After qualifying in 1945 at Birmingham Medical School, becoming an FRCS in 1951 and serving as a general surgeon in the Army and in Stourbridge, he became a pioneering cardiothoracic surgeon who operated at the Queen Elizabeth Hospital and Birmingham Children's Hospital. He developed a heart and lung machine, performed Birmingham's first heart transplant and was highly thought of by his colleagues.

18. Some Distinguished Inhabitants of Rotton Park

LORD MAYORS, COUNCILLORS AND CIVIC OFFICIALS

Sir Wilfrid Martineau MC (1889-1964) and his younger son **Denis** (1920-1999) were the fourth and fifth generations of Martineau males to be Mayor (the first two) or Lord Mayor of Birmingham. Sir Wilfrid, Lord Mayor 1940-41, a solicitor with interests as diverse as the Army and the City of Birmingham Choir, was knighted for his work as Chairman of the City's Education Committee. His wife, **Elvira**, became a Magistrate in 1944 and held several official positions. **Denis** was Lord Mayor 1986-87. They lived at 30 Rotton Park Road.

Walter Samuel Lewis (b.1894), Chairman of the Midlands Electricity Board, was Lord Mayor 1942-43. He lived at 138 Stanmore Road.

Norman Howard Leaker (b.1897), Lord Mayor's Secretary in the 1940s and also one of the founders of the Crescent Theatre, lived at 26 Holly Road.

James Percy Eames MBE, City Treasurer and also Food Officer for Birmingham during World War II, lived at 42 Vernon Road.

John Francis Liverseege, Fellow of the Institute of Chemistry, was the City Analyst and lived at 161 Rotton Park Road. He also ran a local magazine club. Three magazines were passed on during Sundays to the next household on the list and it was my job as a child to deliver last week's magazines to his house. By 1933 he had moved to 12 Jacey Road.

Ernest Cecil West, a City Councillor from 1938 and a member of the Air Raid Precautions Committee, lived at 173 Portland Road.

UNIVERSITY OF BIRMINGHAM

Sir (Harry) Gilbert Barling, Bart. (1855-1940), Vice-Chancellor and Dean of the Faculty of Medicine, lived at 6 Manor Road. (His house was demolished and replaced by a block of flats in 2003.)

Professor R.L.Graeme Ritchie (1880-1954), the University's first Professor of French, who held the post from 1919 until 1944, lived at 10 Manor Road.

Professor Kenneth Neville Moss OBE (1891-1942), Professor of Coal and Metal Mining (did you know that the University had a coal mine?) and Dean of the Faculty of Science, lived at 22 Vernon Road. Sadly, he died at the age of 51.

Professor Brodie Hughes (1913-1989) Professor of Neurosurgery, Dean of the Faculty of Medicine and also an accomplished oboist who played in the University Orchestra, lived at 323 Hagley Road, on the corner of Gillott Road.

Dr Robert Alfred Lambourne (1917-1972) who held degrees in both Medicine and Divinity, ran a course called 'Pastoral Studies' at the University from 1963. He lived at 18 Wheatsheaf Road as a boy and his family and mine were friends.

Peter David Leather, formerly of the University's Centre for Lifelong Learning, an expert on Birmingham although he was born in Liverpool, lived in Gillott Road near the corner of Portland Road when I first knew him. He now lives in France.

Miss Cunningham, who, I am told, was on the staff of the German Faculty, lived in a house on the north side of Melville Road with a very long name-plate on its gate saying 'SCHLAUSCHINKENSCHLOSS', the German for CUNNINGHAM CASTLE.

ORGANISTS

Alfred Robert Gaul (1837-1913), born in Norwich, was appointed as the first Organist of St Augustine's Church in 1868 and stayed there until shortly before his death. He also taught music and was a published composer. He lived in Gillott Road, somewhere near the Hagley Road end, fairly close to the Church.

George Dorrington Cunningham (1878-1948) was City Organist from 1924 until 1948, Conductor of the City of Birmingham Choir from 1926 until 1946 and a Professor of Organ at the Royal Academy of Music in London. He lived at 6 St Augustine's Road.

Thomas William North, born in Walsall in 1883, was appointed Borough Organist of Walsall in 1908 and Organist and Choirmaster of St Augustine's Church in 1919. He lived at 150 City Road and held both appointments until his death in 1955.

David Malcolm Bruce-Payne (b.1945) was Organist and Master of the Choristers at Birmingham Cathedral and Head of Music at King Edward's School from 1974 until 1977. From 1978 until 2003 he was Organist of St George's Church, Edgbaston, and a Senior Lecturer at Birmingham School of Music, which became Birmingham Conservatoire in 1989. He and his wife **Sue**, who was Head of Music at Hallfield School, Edgbaston, lived at 47 Rotton Park Road until 2003, when they retired and went to live in Weymouth.

OTHER MUSICIANS

I know of several City of Birmingham Symphony Orchestra players, past and present, who lived or still live in Rotton Park. These include former Leader **John Georgiadis**, who lived in Selwyn Road during his two years (1965-7) with the CBSO. **Laurence Jackson**, a more recent Leader also lived in Selwyn Road, at number 3. **Enid Beaumont** (violin) lived at 38 Portland Road. **Douglas Milne** (Principal percussion) lived at 140 Rotton Park Road, where his widow, **Betty Milne**, the Town

Hall Manager from 1979 to 1993, still lives. Viola player **Margaret Artus** lived in Moorland Road. **Ruth Gipps**, second oboe and cor anglais in George Weldon's time, lived with her clarinettist husband **Robert Baker** at 102 Portland Road. **Mary Cohen** (violin) lived just within the original boundary of Rotton Park, at 110 Willow Avenue, until a few years ago. She told me that when she was in her back garden she could imagine herself to be in almost any century. A previous owner of the house had been digging in the garden and found a cannon ball dating from the Civil War period and Prince Rupert's Army's charge up Cape Hill!

The sisters **Beatrice** and **Edith Emery**, both Leipzig-trained piano teachers, lived at 7 Vernon Road. Beatrice was my first teacher. **Mary Abbott**, my second teacher and a recitalist, lived 65 Stanmore Road. **Leonard Rayner**, also a piano teacher, lived at 39 Selwyn Road.

Just before the Irish band **Lúnasa** played in the Town Hall in October 2013 there was an article in the *Birmingham Post* about its flautist, **Kevin Crawford**, who, it said, was born in Rotton Park in 1967 to immigrant Irish parents. I got into touch with Kevin, who told me that he had been born at 43 Ashbourne Road, off Rotton Park Road. He left Birmingham in 1989 and now lives in County Clare in Ireland.

MISCELLANEOUS

Joseph Lancaster Ball (1852-1933) was a distinguished architect of the Arts and Crafts period. He designed the Handsworth Wesleyan Theological College in 1889, the house 'Winterbourne' in Edgbaston Park Road for John Nettlefold in 1904 and a pair of semi-detached houses, 17 and 19 Rotton Park Road. He lived at number 17.

The Revd. Dr Rosslyn Bruce (1871-1956), Vicar of St Augustine's from 1912 to 1923, had both a tremendous love of animals (he kept a seal in the Vicarage garden!) and a quirky sense of humour, especially where words were concerned. My sister, who used to attend his Young People's Service on Sunday afternoons, said that he would sometimes bend down in the pulpit and stand up again with a rabbit or a kitten in his hands. When the Botanical Gardens acquired a bear, Dr Bruce named him 'Gladly', after a line from a hymn, 'Gladly the cross I'd bear' (this is what a child thought her parents' were singing).

Dr Rosemary Chrimes, a gold medal-winning athlete now in her eighties, who was awarded an honorary Doctorate by the University of Glasgow, lives at 32 Rotton Park Road.

John Baptist Cramer (formerly Hans von Kramer), a naturalised Briton of German origin, was an inventor well ahead of his time. He used to exhibit his machines at the annual Conversaziones run by the Birmingham and Midland

Institute. I remember one of these (probably in the 1950s) which, if fed with table tennis balls painted pink, yellow or blue, sorted them out into three different columns after each ball had stopped in front of an investigating lamp and the appropriate trapdoor had opened. Not a lot of practical use, you might think, but indicative of much greater electronic marvels to come. He lived at 24 Selwyn Road.

Col. Sir Bertram Ford (1869-1955), Managing Director of *The Birmingham Post and Mail* and also County Commissioner for Birmingham of the St John Ambulance Brigade, lived at 18 Montague Road.

Miss Edith Goodwin, a professional calligrapher who was trained at the Birmingham Municipal School of Art, lived with the Lockies (she was Mrs Lockie's sister) at 29 Wheatsheaf Road. Her beautiful work was known well beyond the bounds of Birmingham.

Sam Harrison founded Birmingham's first Boy Scout troop in 1908. He lived at The Nook, 102 Stanmore Road.

The Revd. William Smith Houghton, Pastor of Francis Road Congregational Church, who married my parents and baptised the three of us, was also Chairman of the Board of Birmingham General Hospital. He lived at 27 Portland Road.

George Spencer Mathews (1836-1904), a land agent, was one of several brothers who were keen mountaineers and founder members of the Alpine Club. He was also Secretary of the Committee which got St Augustine's Church built. He lived at 10 Portland Road.

Orlando Cecil Power (1879-1943), Traffic Manager of the Midland Red Omnibus Company from 1925, lived at 34 Vernon Road. He was known to his family and friends as 'Buddha', which was the nearest his sisters could get to pronouncing the word 'brother' when he was born! We knew him well because my mother had been at school with his wife.

Miss Margery Irene Waterman, for many years Head of the Women's Division of the Birmingham Athletic Institute, lived at 85 Selwyn Road and introduced Ballet to the Institute. She died in 2010, aged 96.

George Henry Wright worked at the Birmingham Chamber of Commerce. His daughter Sylvia told me that as he frequently had to go to London on business, he held a first-class season ticket from Rotton Park Road to London Euston and was the only passenger ever to do so.* He lived at 165 Rotton Park Road, a stone's throw from the station.

Finally, **Hermann Goering** lived at 23 Hallewell Road. However, this was not Hitler's Luftwaffe chief, but another man (originally German) with the same two names. I knew his daughter Anne but I never met him!

* See page 56.

CONCLUSION

The first piece, *'Rotton Park Lodge and the Turner Family'*, which I wrote and illustrated with photos and maps, was an entry for a competition run in 1989 by Barclays Bank and the BBC to celebrate Birmingham's centenary as a city. Entrants had to submit an essay or a scrap-book in an A4 loose-leaf binder on any subject or person(s) connected with Birmingham during the preceding century.

My entry did not win any of the three prizes, the second of which went to Harborne Infants' School, but it was one of ten entries to be 'highly commended'. The authors of the prize-winning and highly commended books were invited to meet the Lord Mayor, Councillor Frederick Chapman, at an exhibition of all the entries at the Central Library on 4 September 1989. I was pleased to find that the group photo taken at my parents' 1908 wedding reception had been taken out of my binder and put up on a display board for all to see. I can identify nearly all of the people on it. It has fascinated everyone to whom I have ever shown it.

But on re-reading my entry recently (I had typed it at some speed and handed it in at BBC Pebble Mill on the last possible day, one hour before entries closed) I realised how many 'facts', particularly dates, I had got wrong in it. I had had to use quite a lot of guesswork to supplement my childhood memories and the documents and photos which I then possessed. For instance, I did not discover Stanton Marsh's name until considerably later.

My final piece for the University's 'Birmingham Studies' course was a 6,000-word (plus or minus 10%) illustrated essay entitled *'Rotton Park Lodge and the Farm'*. It was marked by Peter Leather and an external assessor. It was also produced against the clock on a typewriter, so I was unable to do any subsequent editing or pruning. When I was running very close to the maximum of 6,600 words I realised that I still had important things to write about my own family for which there was going to be no room, so I admit that Peter's comment 'Ends a bit abruptly!' was justified. However, I did get an 'A' for it.

I did a great deal more study, local visiting and exploration before writing this book, which has taken me a ***very*** long time. As I was by now using a computer it was possible for me to edit and make alterations as I went along. I have checked my facts carefully, but if you know that I am wrong on any point, please do write to me, c/o Brewin Books Ltd, 56 Alcester Road, Studley, Warwickshire, B70

8NP. I have been able to visit Rotton Park only rarely since I gave up driving some years ago. I have tried to keep up-to-date with any major changes there, though I realise that I may have missed a few of them.

The photos of the houses built in the 1930s in Rotton Park Road and Wheatsheaf Road were taken in 2009 by my professional photographer friend Fritz Curzon, who has also prepared many of the older photos for publication. My sincere thanks go to him for his excellent work.

I am also grateful to Professor Roger Ward, an experienced author, for reading through my text and making many helpful suggestions and to my architect friend Ann Levitt for her plans (she told me that she had enjoyed the challenge of constructing them). So many other people have helped me in different ways over the years that I cannot list them individually, but I do thank all of them.

On my 94th birthday in July 2013 I was taken by my goddaughter Sarah Bond on a tour of nearly all of the roads in Rotton Park, including the new ones off City Road between Shenstone Road and Portland Road which I had not seen before.

I do know, of course, and regret that Rotton Park acquired a 'different' reputation some years ago, which led to one end of some of its roads being closed to motor traffic. Draw your own conclusions about how this change was able to come about.

A fairly new block of flats at 2 Rotton Park Road is now called 'The Lodge'. Well, as **our** Lodge was demolished in 1934, I suppose the name was quite fairly up for grabs. But to me 'The Lodge' will always mean Rotton Park Lodge, a name which brings back memories of the happy childhood days which I spent living next door to my Turner grandparents and being allowed to play in their lovely garden.

Conclusion

The author celebrating her 95th birthday.

The author up the cedar of Lebanon.